Reviews

"A compelling look at Justice gone awry..."

"A fascinating look at the inner workings of a jury in a serious criminal case,
And an indictment of the system that has been shown, too often,
To convict the innocent..."

- Deuce Niven, Tabor/Loris Tribune

"A Real Eye Opener"

"Should be required reading for students at all levels, especially law school...

Criminal defense attorneys and judges shouldn't be able to try a case
Until they have read this book..."

- Ebook-Reviews

"Highly recommend it to everyone and especially those who are called
Or subject to being called for jury duty." – J. Clark

"I can only hope I am never asked to be a juror...
A very compelling story with a life changing ending..."
– P. Joines

J.L. Hardee

JUSTICE OR INJUSTICE?
WHAT REALLY HAPPENS IN A JURY ROOM

J. L. Hardee

Copyright 2011, Print Edition

J.L. Hardee

On June 9, 1998, William Brent Poole was murdered on a dark beach, in Myrtle Beach, SC. Within days of his death, his wife and her ex-lover, were arrested and charged with his murder.

Kimberly Renee Poole was charged with murder, and conspiracy to commit murder for allegedly conspiring with her former lover, John Boyd Frazier to kill her husband.

In November 1999, the capital murder trial of Kimberly Renee Poole began in Conway, SC.

I was a juror on that trial and this is my story.

One could only imagine what it's like to serve on a jury. No one could ever imagine what it's like to serve on a capital murder trial. Ever wonder what being on a jury is like? Ever wonder what goes on in a jury room? This is....

WHAT REALLY HAPPENS IN A JURY ROOM!

J.L. Hardee

Disclaimer

This story is based on actual events that took place in NC and SC. The events portrayed in this book are based solely from the author's memory and perception. The facts listed are from the view point of the author and are not meant to reflect the view point of any other person. The names of agents from the SC Law Enforcement Division, aka SLED, have been changed to protect their identity. Other names used are of real persons and places.

J.L. Hardee

Special Thanks to:

my Mom for standing by me through thick and thin

and

my 12th grade English teacher, who made me pay attention in class.

For more books by J L Hardee and for updates visit:

http://www.amazon.com/J.L.-Hardee

https://www.smashwords.com/profile/view/hardeejl

https://www.facebook.com/J.L.HARDEE.AUTHOR

J.L. Hardee

FORETHOUGHT

This story is based on actual events that took place in Horry County, South Carolina, 1998-99.

This story involves a murder that took place in Myrtle Beach, SC, and the trial of one of the accused, Kimberly Renee Poole.

I was a Juror in the case of The State of SC vs. Kimberly Renee Poole, and this is my story.

When reading this story, I ask that you keep a few things in mind....

    * I am by no means a professional author.

    * I am trying to provide you with an accurate account of what really happens during jury deliberations.

    * The innocence or guilt of this defendant is not the point of this story.

    * This story is not about me or the small town I grew up in.

    * Do you believe in our Justice system?

J.L. Hardee

* Do you believe that people receive fair trials in our system of justice?

* Is it possible to send an innocent person to prison?

After reading this story, I think you will change your views of our justice system, and it will bring the cold, hard, scary truth to light. Do you want your fate in the hands of twelve jurors?

CHAPTER I

I am not writing this book for me and it is not about me. Though, for you to understand what really took place, you may need to know a little bit about me.

I was born and raised in Horry County, SC. I went to school in the small town of Loris. Loris is a quaint town where everyone knows everybody, and everyone knows your business. I was no genius. I may have graduated with a 2.5 GPA from Loris High School. I am just an average Joe from a small town in the middle of nowhere. Most people that grow up there do everything they can to leave and never return. Unless you own your own small town mom or pop business, there aren't many jobs. I never wanted to leave though.

All I ever wanted to be growing up was a Firefighter like my father. I never aspired to be rich or famous. As a firefighter, you are faced with great responsibilities every day and you take on the privilege of protecting others and holding their lives in your hands at some times. That was a burden that I was ready and willing for.

J.L. Hardee

Holding the fate of someone's life in your hands is very tricky, and, when it comes to being a juror, it was something that I had never thought of, never imagined, and was not prepared for.

CHAPTER II

The day that would forever change my life began just like any other day. I was on a day off from the Fire Department and working with my father building houses. Firefighting never paid enough to live off of, and, as a newlywed and a new father, I had to work hard to support my family. I was just twenty-two years old. I was not very sophisticated and not very smart, so it was going to take a lot of hard work to make it in this world and be able to provide a good life for my wife and child.

When one is twenty-two years old, they don't think about the consequences of all of their decisions. They don't think about what happens if…. They never think about having the fate of someone's life in their hands as a juror on a capital murder trial.

At twenty-two, as a young male, all I thought about was work, fishing, sex and my son, and not necessarily in that order. The future and how my decisions affected my future was something that never crossed my mind.

J.L. Hardee

I started work that day just like any other at 6 a.m., and my only thoughts were toward making plans for the upcoming weekend and when I might get to go fishing. We always started work early between 6 or 7 a.m., depending on day light. We had a pretty regular routine. At 9:30 every morning, we took a break, which meant we usually went to Cox's Convenience store for a sausage dog and a Pepsi. That day was no different. The only difference was my dad decided to go to the post office to pick up his mail.

I sat on a stack of plywood and chatted with other employees when my dad pulled back up at the job site. I think he always liked scaring me a bit or providing extra drama to see my reaction.

When he got out of the truck, he said, "boy, what have you got into now?"

"What?" I said.

He said, "You have a notice from the clerk of court here". "There's a letter at the post office for you that requires your signature."

"What?" I said again. "What does that mean? Who is it from? Why would they be sending me a letter? I haven't done anything wrong. Are you sure it's from the clerk of court? What is the clerk of court?" I bet I asked him fifty questions all at once.

He said, "I don't know…the only way you will find out is to go get the letter."

J.L. Hardee

I got in the truck immediately. My curiosity got the best of me. As I pulled out of the drive, my dad said, "It's probably a notice for jury duty."

I hit the brake immediately and just as abruptly as I pulled out, I pulled back in.

"Jury Duty?"

"Why would I be getting a notice for jury duty? I'm not old enough to serve on a jury. Am I? I don't want to serve on a jury. Why would they want me to serve on a jury? How would they know how to contact me?"

My dad chimed in again and said, "Didn't you use my address when you registered to vote? I think that's how they choose jurors. I think they send out random notices to registered voters."

"Well, what do I do? Do I have to do it? Do I have to go get the letter??

"No, you don't have to but if you don't and it's for jury duty, they may come looking for you."

"What should I do?"

"Go get the letter and just see what it is and then we can go from there", he said.

"Ok."

I decided to wait for lunch before I went to the post office. I was no longer in a hurry, and my curiosity turned to fear. The next two hours were very long in one stance and also very short. I couldn't get my mind off of that letter. Those two hours went by way too fast in the end. I thought we would have lunch first and stop by the post office on our way back to work. Not so. I think my dad's curiosity was stronger than mine. He drove us straight to the post office at noon that day. I didn't want to get out of the truck. I sat there biting my finger nails and smoking a cigarette. A usually calm morning and boring day at work soon turned into a stressful event.

"Get your butt out of this truck, go get that letter, and see what it is." He wasn't going to let me forget about it.

I finally got out and went in. In our little town, the post office employees know us when we walk in. We don't have to tell them our names and what we are there for.

As soon as I walked in, the postal employee said, "I have a letter for you. You have to sign for it."

"What is it? Who is it from?"

"It's from the Horry County Clerk of Court, they have been sending out notices for jury duty for next week."

"For what?"

"I think there's a big murder trial from the beach coming up."

J.L. Hardee

"Murder trial? We don't have murders around here. Who got murdered? When?"

"I don't know. I think it's a murder trial from something that happened at the beach last year".

"I don't want to serve on a murder trial. What happens if I don't sign for it? Do I have to sign for it?"

"You have to for me to give it to you. I can return it undeliverable for you".

"Yea, do that. Just send it back to them as if you couldn't reach me. You will do that?"

"Sure, no problem."

Ok. I weaseled out of that. My mind was at ease again. The post office would just send it back like they couldn't reach me. *I won't have to serve on a jury. I'm surely not serving on a murder trial.*

Back in those days, the Internet wasn't really big in our small town. Yes, I knew what it was. I wasn't that far in the sticks, but it just hadn't hit really big yet. Computers hadn't either. I didn't have a computer, much less the Internet, and there surely weren't any IPods to access the net with. There was no way for me to research or look into what was going on. My small town was full of gossip, and I could have inquired through the gossip mill, but that would do me no good because in my small town we don't care about anyone else. We only talk about our

J.L. Hardee

own. If they weren't one of us, they didn't have to worry about us talking about them. We didn't keep up with the Kardashians. If they weren't from our neck of the woods, we didn't care about them or what they were doing. The only news I kept up with was our local newspaper, owned by my cousin. It was the Loris Scene. The paper came out only once a week, and murders rarely if any ever crossed the lines of that paper. News from the beach wasn't news to us. We didn't care what happened at the beach. That was a whole different world, even though it was only twenty miles away.

I continued with my weekend as if nothing else was going on. I spent my time playing with my wife and son and never thought about that jury notice again.

I went to work at the Fire Department that Sunday just like it was another day at work. I was hoping to catch a structure fire. I really enjoyed the adrenaline rush of fighting fires. The action and excitement really consumed me. The dangers never crossed my mind. I was young and dumb, with no thoughts of what if.

I started my day out checking my fire engine and gossiping with my fellow firefighters. It was a Sunday. We didn't really do much work on Sunday unless we got a call. The day was going by pretty uneventfully. After completing our listing of morning duties, we retired to the day room for breakfast and a break. We were all in the dayroom watching

J.L. Hardee

television when a deputy sheriff walked in. I didn't think anything of it. The police hang out with us all the time. It's usually county police and not sheriff's deputies though, but that didn't ring a bell with me at the time.

In Horry County, things are a little different than in most counties. They have two law-enforcement agencies in the county. Political corruption with previous Sheriffs prompted the county to waste a lot more tax dollars and pay two senior law enforcement department heads instead of one. Rather than fixing the problem, they did what most government officials do; they put a band-aid on it, and decided to have two completely separate police departments for one jurisdiction. I thought elections were for getting rid of corrupt politicians or corrupt Sheriffs. Not in Horry County, SC. They just make an entirely new police department.

Anyway, the deputy came in and sat down like he was just one of the guys. I didn't know him personally, but I knew who he was and I knew he knew me. He made his rounds with the "hellos" and the "how are you doing", and after conversing with everyone, he got up as if he was going to leave.

When he stood up, he looked at me. "I have something for you," he said.

"Hum? What is it?"

J.L. Hardee

"Here you are. You have been officially served with jury notification. You have to report to the courthouse tomorrow morning at 8:30 a.m. sharp. Don't be late."

"What if I get held over or have a fire?"

"You better not be late", he said and left as fast as he snuck in.

That sneaky devil! Damn, they must want me badly. They had a deputy serve me at work on a Sunday. "What the heck? What is so important that they have to track me down at work on a Sunday for?"

My captain weighed in. "You must be serving on that capital murder trial."

"You mean they are going to really make me serve on a jury? I don't want to serve on a jury. I have no business being on a jury. I don't know anything about juries."

"Well, if you want to get out of it, just show up to court wearing your uniform. I doubt they'll pick you to be on the jury if you do that".

"Ok! That sounds good. I'm just getting off of work then and I will have to go by there before I go home. I won't have time to go home and change anyway."

"No, I'm going to get you some relief in here early so you make sure you're on time and don't get in trouble for being late. It wouldn't look good for a county employee showing up late for jury duty".

J.L. Hardee

CHAPTER III

I didn't sleep a wink that night. Between the rhymes of all the snoring in our shared bunk room and the thoughts of a capital murder trial running through my head, who could sleep? It was a long night. Tossing and turning, getting up and down, going out to smoke and biting off all of my fingernails is the best I can describe it.

Some may think that I'm making this more dramatic than it should have been or blowing it out of proportion. This was dramatic. It was big for the small town where I grew up. At Loris High, they warned me that I may run into bad guys one day, or I may be asked to use drugs. Our biggest warning was not to get anyone pregnant. They never taught us about the law. Law courses weren't offered between our country English and math classes. We didn't have Law 101.

Sex-Ed was the most unusual class we had. We were never taught that one day we may have to serve on a jury; it's our responsibility as citizens, or what it would be like. We were never told that one day we may be faced with having to decide the fate of someone's life. I was very ill-prepared for what was to come.

I laid awake in bed for the last hour. We always woke at about 6 a.m. to clean up and get ready for the next shift. When the alarm went off at 6, I was in the shower already. I pressed my uniform, buffed my boots, and even brushed my teeth. I wanted to look my best and I hoped I stood out in my uniform. Boy did I.

The captain had my relief arrive at 7 a.m. Not that we had to worry about any calls. It was just my luck; it was a dry shift with no action to keep my mind off of the pending court appearance. I arrived early at about 7:45. My captain wasn't going to let me be late. I sat in my pickup truck and chain-smoked until I saw what appeared to be other people arriving for jury duty. I entered the courthouse with my head held high, poking my chest out, trying to draw attention to the badge on my chest.

A court deputy was just beyond the door with a note pad. "Are you here for jury duty?" He asked.

"Yes, here is my notice."

"Just go have a seat in that room."

Over two hundred people showed up for that jury duty. At around 9 a.m., the deputy came in and escorted us all into a very large courtroom. We all sat in the gallery and waited, for what seemed like hours.

Just a few moments later though, we heard the Bailiff yell....

J.L. Hardee

"All rise! This honorable court, in and for Horry County, SC, is now in session, the Honorable Edward Cottingham presiding."

The judge began by thanking us all for showing up to do our civic duty as jurors and then began telling us what was going to happen over the next few hours. He told us that we were here for a capital murder trial which may involve the death penalty. He stated the reasons that a juror could be excused. He went down the list. He said, "If any of the following applies to you, I want you to Stand, and come up front. If you're a police officer or someone in your immediate family is, if you're a school teacher, or if you've been convicted of a felony, please come forward.

Hum? Well, none of that applied to me. Maybe he'll get me next. About a third of the room rose and went forward. It took awhile to dismiss those jurors. He asked them one by one to state their conflict. *My husband is a police officer. I'm married to a police officer. I am a school teacher. I have a felony conviction.* One by one they went up and had to state their reasons in open court.

What happened to privacy? It goes straight out the door when you're called before the court during jury selections.

After dismissing all of those jurors, the judge added some additional reasons that we could be dismissed. *If you have any hardships, are single parents, have any medical conditions, elderly, and so on.*

J.L. Hardee

None of the excuses fit me. *What about firefighters?* I wondered. Those last conditions cleared most of the room and left us with only about 25-30 people. Out of about two hundred that was all who were left.

I was sure they would excuse me soon. I had to be standing out. I was the only one seated in the gallery who was in a uniform. Guess what?

"Sir, please rise and come forward." The judge stated, looking directly at me.

I think my knees were shattering. I walked forward with my head held high. I remember thinking, this is it for me. I am done with this.

"Sir, where do you work?"

"For Horry County Fire Department," I stated.

"Are you working today?"

"No your honor; I just got off from my shift."

"Good, I want you to go home, change clothes, and be back by 1 p.m. You don't have any hardships that would prevent you from being on this jury, do you?"

I thought really hard. I looked through my little mind for any excuse I could come up with.

"No, your honor!"

J.L. Hardee

I was too scared to give him a bullshit excuse, and I couldn't come up with anything good. I thought about telling him that I was the sole provider for my family and that I needed to work, but I am sure he was aware, as I was, that the county paid its employees when they had to serve on jury duty. That wasn't going to fly. I was going to get my regular pay check whether I was in court or at work.

I left the courthouse that day still feeling confident that I wouldn't be picked. I said to myself, *there's no way the defense is going to want a county employee, much less a firefighter on the jury.*

CHAPTER IV

"Honey, I'm home. Do I have any clean dress clothes?"

"Why?" My wife, Kelly asked.

"I have to go back to court for jury duty. I didn't get dismissed yet. The judge told me to come home and change clothes and be back after lunch."

My son, Justin, had just turned two years old the week prior to this trial, and if I didn't get out of jury duty, I was going to be spending my birthday doing that. I spent a little time playing with my son while my wife kindly searched for clothes for me to wear. She returned with a pair of khaki pants, with just a few wrinkles and a golf shirt. That was about as dressy as I got.

"Will this do?" Kelly asked.

"I guess so. A lot of people were wearing jeans. I just want to look nice. I doubt I'll be there long though. I'm sure they are going to dismiss me. I showed up in uniform."

J.L. Hardee

I thought I would be back home by 3 p.m. at the latest. As I drove back to the courthouse, I wasn't even thinking about the pending trial or what if I was picked. I planned for dinner, and what I was going to do at work with my dad the next day.

When I arrived, the courthouse was a lot less chaotic. There were only about 20 Jurors left. They had dismissed some others while I was gone.

"They have to have at least 12, right?" I asked someone.

"No, they have to have some alternates too."

"What? How many of those do they need?"

"They will need at least two, maybe more."

I began sweating and getting nervous again. I'm surprised I still had any fingers left to gnaw on. I kept saying, *Ok, they don't have to have all of us, I'll be one of the few left to be let go.*

The judge asked us all to leave the room and follow the bailiff. He escorted us to an adjacent room and told us to just wait in here until he came back for us. One by one, they called us back into the courtroom. I was about the tenth person called in. When I walked back into the courtroom, the judge asked me to take a seat in the witness box. I had to be sworn in. The judge asked me a few questions and then gave me the details surrounding the murder case.

J.L. Hardee

He said, "We're here for a murder trial. "The death penalty is no longer being sought, so you don't have to worry about that. Do you have any knowledge of this case?"

"No, your honor." I replied.

"Ok, the attorneys are going to ask you some questions now."

"Ok."

Do you want to be on this jury? That wasn't a question that was ever placed before me. A definite *No* would have been my answer. It has been well over ten years since the trial so I can't remember all of their questions. They were all pretty simple though.

"Do you know the defendant? Do you know the judge, or any of the attorneys? Have you read about this case any?"

I answered a simple "no" to all the questions. Then the defense attorney asked me more personal questions and I began thinking, *yea, it's about time*.

"Do you work for the fire department? How long have you been there? What area of the county do you work? Have you ever worked in Myrtle Beach? Has any other county employees discussed this case with you?"

Nothing seemed to help me. Nothing applied to me. The final question and one that will haunt me forever....

J.L. Hardee

"Do you think you can be fair and impartial and decide this case based on the evidence or the lack of evidence presented to you?"

"Yes, I can!"

I didn't even know it at the time, but I'd just perjured myself. The biggest question they posed to me was the one question that could have saved me, gotten me removed from the jury, and I lied to myself, to the court, to the defense attorney, and to the defendant when I said, "yes I can."

"He is acceptable to the defense your honor." Defense Attorney William Diggs stated.

"Any objections from the prosecution?" The judge asked.

"No."

"Sir, you are now part of this jury. You'll be sequestered from now until the end of this trial. We'll allow you time to go home and pack some bags. You'll need to pack enough clothes to last you about 2 weeks. You can go home now. Do not discuss this case with anyone. Go pack your bags and come right back. You'll be staying at a motel in the area. You'll be able to have monitored phone calls with just your wife and kids. You won't be allowed any visitors or be allowed to receive phone calls. You can't tell anyone where you will be staying."

What the hell? My lord, who did this girl kill? Did she kill the president? What is with all this nonsense?

J.L. Hardee

I wasn't brave enough to say those thoughts aloud. My brain continued to run wild though. I have to be away from my wife and son for two weeks? I have to go without sex for two weeks? You think that's funny. I thought about it. I was a 22-year-old man in my prime. Two weeks without sex was like a death sentence to me. *What am I going to eat for two weeks? I don't like fast-food. I'm a country boy, and I grew up eating home-cooked meals. I'm going to be away from home for two weeks.* Those thoughts consumed me the entire drive home. I couldn't even talk my wife into making love before I had to leave.

I didn't have many dress clothes. I packed jeans, golf shirts, one nice pair of dress pants, and the matching dress shirt. I called my dad and my Fire Captain and told them the bad news and that was it.

That was how my life and my innocent view of the world were forever changed.

J.L. Hardee

CHAPTER V

I arrived back at the courthouse that evening around 6 p.m. It was dinner time for us country folks. That's when I got to meet all of my fellow jurors for the first time. It wasn't really a meeting or introduction time though. None of us spoke to each other. We all stood there outside the courthouse and just waited.

A deputy showed up and with a list in hand, he called out our names. "Ok, you're all here. From here on out, you're going to be sequestered. You'll travel with security everywhere you go. These gentleman and lady are from the SC State Law Enforcement Division, and they'll be with you until the end of this trial. If you have any questions or need anything, you just let them know."

I never saw a SLED agent before. I heard of them, but they were rarely seen in our neck of the woods. I had no idea what their jobs entailed. *This must be really serious if they have the state police guarding us,* I thought.

J.L. Hardee

We were all given the option of leaving our vehicles at the courthouse or taking them with us to the motel. I chose to take mine. It appeared that it would be the last time I was alone for some time. We all piled into our vehicles and one by one were led in a motorcade fashion to the motel, with a deputy in front of us and in the rear. It was like something I'd seen on television. We were escorted to one of the newer motels on Highway 501 in the Carolina Forest area. For those who know where I am talking about, Carolina Forest was still a forest. All of the restaurants, shops and fancy neighborhoods hadn't arrived yet. We were kind of in hiding.

When we arrived at the motel, we were told that we had just enough time to drop off our bags, and then we would all be going out for dinner. We didn't have to check in. The rooms were already booked and not in our names. They had the entire second floor indoors secured for this jury and the accompanying SLED agents. At least, we all had our own rooms. For a minute, I thought we would have to share a room with someone else. I didn't realize the expense the county or the state went to having a jury sequestered. We weren't allowed any time to admire our new living quarters. We dropped our bags in the rooms and were given time to have a potty break before we all gathered back in the lobby. They had two large 15-passenger, church style vans waiting for us when we walked back outside. Our vehicles were parked for the duration.

J.L. Hardee

I could only imagine what they were going to feed us. McDonald's was my thought at the time. I hated fast-food and that was irking me. *Those tiny burgers that tasted like soybeans and we were mostly bread. Those shoestring fries that are only tolerable straight out of the fryer, which they never are. You mine as well order two slices of bread with ketchup.* They didn't bother to ask us where we wanted to eat that night, and none of us had a clue where we were going. I was really surprised when we pulled up at a Steak and Seafood restaurant. The restaurant was already prepared for us. We had a private room off to ourselves. It obviously wasn't a last-minute decision on where we were going to eat. Some pre-planning had gone into that.

We all sat down at a large table together. No one was off to themselves. Finally, one of the agents spoke to us. I thought they were robots up to that point.

"Ya'll order whatever you want, it's on us."

Hum! Whatever I want? They must be kidding, I thought. I began looking at the menu. Ribeyes, prime rib, seafood platter....All looks good, but it was kind of expensive. I started looking for the cheaper meals thinking that they weren't really serious about us ordering whatever we wanted. Then I heard one of the SLED agents order the prime rib and then a juror ordered a seafood platter. Those were $18 - $20 plates. I was use to ordering something $10 or less when I went out to eat. I thought… *this is going to be a real treat.* It was. I ordered the prime rib as well. I ordered it rare. Just the way I liked it. With a loaded baked potato and a side salad, it was a nice meal. We all ate in silence that night. I can't remember anyone speaking to each other. The first thing I remember is one of the older gentlemen asking, "Can we get dessert?"

"Sure, we just have to make it quick. You all have a long day ahead of you tomorrow."

Now you know how your tax dollars are really spent and why a trial costs so much.

We all ordered desert. Some ordered it just because they could. I ordered desert knowing that I didn't have room for it. I was a mere 175lbs. At 6'3" tall, I was a stick. The prime rib was enough to fill me without the potato and salad. I ordered it anyway. Chocolate cake was my choice. I remember I only took two bites of it. My pants were about to pop already. I had them package the desert to go as if I would have the chance to eat it later.

After dinner, we all loaded back into the vans and headed to the motel. Still unsure of exactly what we were supposed to be doing. It was a long, silent ride back to the motel. We could have heard a pin drop. I guess everyone was scared to be the first to speak. It was dead silence. As we exited the vans, an agent told us that we would all be gathering in

J.L. Hardee

one of the rooms upstairs for a meeting, and they would tell us the rules we all had to follow. Upstairs, the agents had turned two adjoining motel rooms into kind of a dayroom. The beds had been removed, and there were two televisions and enough chairs for all of us. We all gathered in the room quietly as if we were in trouble or something. We were sitting there waiting for someone to speak.

One agent finally spoke up. "My name is James Long and I am a special agent with the South Carolina Law Enforcement Division, also known as SLED. I'm the agent in charge and if you have any questions or concerns, you can ask me or one of my fellow agents."

He then introduced his fellow agents. There were four of them. There were three gentlemen and one female agent.

"Here are some rules that you will all have to follow while you are serving on this jury. First, you aren't allowed to discuss this case with us or amongst yourselves at all. We can't answer any questions about the case for you. You will all have your own rooms and you will be required to stay in your rooms after 10 p.m. until we wake you up the following morning."

Immediately, I raised my hand.

"Yes Sir?"

"Are we allowed to smoke in the rooms?"

"Yes, you'll be allowed to smoke in your rooms, because you are not allowed to go outside at all without an escort and only then if it's something important. You will not be allowed any outside contact with your family or friends. You can make one phone call each evening to your significant other, and that phone call will be monitored by an agent. You are not allowed to tell your family where you are or discuss any of the jurors, agents or this case. This is the community room where you can all hang out, but you aren't allowed to talk about anything related to this case. You will be allowed to watch television, but no news, crime shows, and nothing with any violence. One of the agents will pick what you can watch and you are not allowed to turn the television, so don't ask. You'll all be woken up at 5:30 a.m. and we'll all go to breakfast together, leaving here no later than 6:30 a.m. So, that gives you an hour to get ready. If you need longer, there are alarm clocks in your rooms. If you didn't notice, the televisions and the phones have been removed from your rooms, so you won't be getting any wake up calls from the front desk. If any of you have cell phones, I need you to pass them up. They will be returned to you after the end of this trial."

Damn, they're serious. It was like we were in jail. Our every move was controlled.

"Finally, if you have any ideas for places to eat dinner, you can let one of the agents know and we will see if it can be done. We'll be eating breakfast at the same place each morning, and your lunch will be brought to you at the courthouse. The only difference will be that we can eat dinner at different places if they have private dining areas. Now, are there any questions?"

No one spoke up. I think I was the only idiot that asked a question that evening, and it was if I could smoke cigarettes in my room.

"Ok, you will all be allowed to call home, but make it quick, we have 14 people that have to use the phone."

My phone call was to my wife, Kelly. I remember telling her, "Honey, I made it to hell. I can't talk on the phone or watch television until this is over. I can't tell you where I am, but we have checked in and I am okay. I will call you tomorrow night. I love you. Good night!" It was short and sweet. She didn't even ask me anything. I was kind of nervous when I got off the phone wondering if an agent had been listening in and had heard me say that I made it to hell, but no one ever said anything to me. They obviously weren't monitoring our calls as closely as I thought they would be, or they just didn't care about what I had said.

After we were all done with our phone calls, Agent Long spoke to us again. He said, "You won't have a key to your rooms, you'll all be escorted to and from your rooms at all times. First, an agent will need to go with you to your rooms and search your bags before we allow you to go in for the night."

I jumped up quickly to be the first, because I was ready for a smoke.

The agent led me to my room and came in behind me. "Where are your bags?"

"That one on the bed is the only one I brought."

"Ok, let me look in it. You don't have any weapons do you?"

"No!" I thought, *isn't that a question they should have asked us earlier?*

"Ok, you're good. If you need to leave the room or speak to an agent, just knock on your door and wait for someone to come to you."

That was it. I was there for the night. We had a small refrigerator in our rooms with an assortment of sodas and water. There was an ashtray on the table by the window. It was all I needed with exception of a television. It was getting late by this point, though, and I really didn't even care about watching television. I took a shower and went straight to bed. To my surprise, I slept like a baby all night. I woke up to an agent knocking on my door the next morning.

J.L. Hardee

CHAPTER VI

It only took me fifteen minutes to get ready the next morning. After a nice hot shower, I threw my clothes on, and I was ready for work. The excitement of what was to begin started hitting me. I wasn't scared anymore. I was really nervous, excited, and anxious to see what all of the drama was about. As soon as I was dressed, I knocked on my door. An agent came by. I asked, "Where is the coffee?"

"You have a pot in your room, or there's some in the day room. Are you ready to come out?"

I stepped out and the agent directed me to the day room where one of the agents was sitting watching cartoons with another juror. I hadn't even noticed the coffeepot in my room. They really prepared for this. There were three large coffeepots in the dayroom and I helped myself to a cup.

I was forced to watch Bugs Bunny for the next half hour or so while we waited on the other jurors. Of course, the women took the longest.

All of the men were in the dayroom watching cartoons while the ladies took their time.

When the last female juror was ready, we were quickly taken downstairs to the vans that were waiting on us. They were parked at the front door with additional deputies standing by. Again, I thought, *damn this is serious*. We have our own private security and a full detail at that. I remembered them saying that the places we ate at had to have a private dining room, so I wasn't afraid of having to eat McDonald's for breakfast. We were taken to a private diner on the west side of Conway, the opposite side of town from where we were staying. When I walked in, I was amazed. They had a full course buffet laid out just for us. There was bacon, smoked sausage, linked sausage, sausage patties, corned beef hash, scrambled eggs, grits, hash browns, and my favorite, biscuits and gravy. Everything a country boy could want.

We all gorged ourselves on the feast before us. It was like we were on vacation. We could have anything and all we wanted of it. We didn't even have to leave a tip. I remember thinking after I was done eating that it probably wasn't smart to eat that much, I would want a nap in an hour or so.

Dessert wasn't offered to us that morning. I think it was the only thing missing. They even brought fruit out for one female juror that appeared to be watching her figure. She should have started watching it long before then, because she appeared to weigh more than I did.

CHAPTER VII

We arrived at the Horry County Court at 8:30 a.m. that morning. We were allowed to take a smoke break before we went inside, and then we were taken to a small room, that didn't seem much larger than a jail cell. It definitely was smaller than our motel rooms. There was one large table with a lot of chairs around it. They had coffee, water and sodas in the corner of the room for us. At the end of the room was a small door, and we were told that was our only restroom and that we had to share it. There wasn't enough space in the room to really walk around. We had to all sit down. Dead silence is all I remembered from the other jurors that morning. We all sat there waiting to be told what was next. At 9 a.m. the deputy came in and told us that court would be starting soon and that we would all wait here until the judge called for us.

"Do any of you want a pad of paper and a pen to take notes? You can't use your own. We'll provide that for you."

Only a few of us raised our hands. I was among them. I didn't know if I'd need it or if I'd take notes, but I decided to take it when it was

J.L. Hardee

offered to me. I had not even thought about having to take notes. It was like we were in a class at school.

At around 9:15 that morning, the bailiff came for us, and we all went into the courtroom single file.

Wow! The court room was packed, and there were television crews with cameras. I had never seen anything like this. My nerves hit me again. Everyone was watching us. All eyes in that court room followed us to our seats. I looked around scanning the room. There were all sorts of people, ranging from old to young, from well-dressed to your average country man wearing jeans and flannel shirt. There were Sheriff's deputies everywhere. All of the entrances were guarded. *Who is this person? Is she someone famous? Did she kill someone famous?* I thought. At this point, I had no idea. Some of the jurors may have known what we were there for, but I didn't yet.

As we sat down, the judge greeted us with a 'good morning', and 'thank you for being here to serve on this jury'. Then he began to tell us why we were all there. The details of the case were then explained to us.

"You're here to hear evidence in the case of The State of SC vs. Kimberly Renee Poole. The Defendant is sitting at the far table and the people with her are her defense attorneys. At the table next to you is the State's attorney's. The defendant is charged with two counts, murder and conspiracy to commit murder. She's accused of conspiring to kill

J.L. Hardee

her husband. The defendant is presumed innocent until you the jury have heard all of the evidence, and having heard that evidence; make a finding of guilt or innocence."

The judge continued with some instructions as to what would take place, informing us that we would be listening to open arguments from the prosecution and the defense that morning. He told us that we would take a break at around 10:30, and then we would break for lunch around noon.

"Does anyone need anything before we begin?"

No one spoke up.

"Is the prosecution ready? Is the defense ready?"

"Yes your honor", said both and then it began.

The Prosecution's opening statements were given by Deputy Solicitor Fran Humphries. Mr. Humphries was a very average-looking guy that appeared to be in his mid 30's. He was well dressed, polite, and spoke with a familiar country twang. He was a good choice for the State to represent them. It was obvious as soon as he began speaking that Mr. Humphries was an experienced public speaker and was doing what he was meant for. He began speaking to us in a polite, quiet voice, and as he walked us through his theory of the case and the evidence that would be presented to us, he gradually raised his tone to provide some extra drama and suspense to the case.

J.L. Hardee

I was paying very close attention to Mr. Humphries. It wasn't because I was supposed to or because he was the district attorney. I was just curious to know what all the circus and drama was about and who this defendant was to warrant such. *Who is she? Who did she kill? Why is this case and this person warranting so much media attention and police protection?* I thought.

While listening to his explanation as to why we were there, I never got a good answer for the questions running through my mind. Apparently, this young lady was just your average person, and she just killed her average husband.

There wasn't a good reason for all the drama and expense that they had put us and the citizens of the community through.

CHAPTER VIII

Kimberly Renee Poole was a 23 year old, Caucasian female from Winston-Salem, NC. She was no one special. She was married to Brent Poole, your average Caucasian guy from Winston-Salem too. These people weren't presidents. They weren't movie stars. They weren't wealthy, high society people. Well, then why all the hype? I never got an answer to that, and I still don't understand it.

Of course it's terrible what happened, and it's terrible when anyone is murdered, but this case just didn't warrant all the hype.

We were told that Kimberly Renee Poole had been married to Brent Poole for a couple of years, and they had one child together, a daughter that was about 2 years old. They had had a rocky marriage that included some adultery on the part of Mrs. Poole. This extra-marital affair began while Mrs. Poole was employed as a stripper at a local night club in Winston-Salem. At some point during their marriage, the Poole's suffered some financial setbacks and at the insistence of Brent Poole, Kimberly Renee Poole took a job as a stripper to support her family.

J.L. Hardee

The Poole's became swingers, bringing home girls to have extra-marital relations with. This was done at the suggestion of the husband, Brent Poole.

Wow! This was the first I have ever heard of anything like this. I grew up in the sticks. I never thought about having an extra woman with my wife. I was astonished. They had my attention. The story was getting interesting.

Well, at some point during all of this, Mrs. Poole began a relationship with John Boyd Frasier, whom she met while working as a stripper. I didn't think much of this. Her husband was getting extra girls. So in my mind, she was entitled to an extra guy. They weren't really clear on what the arrangement was with all of this extra play during their marriage. I take it though that the husband was being selfish and didn't approve of extra men, just extra women. The exact details of what happened and how the relationship went south I believe was just speculation on anyone's part. I don't think anyone really knew the details of what really happened. Only two or three people did, and they weren't speaking.

After some time though, the Poole's began having problems with their arrangement and began fighting. Kimberly Renee Poole moved in with John Boyd Frasier in a continuation of their love affair. This really frustrated her husband, and he began making threats towards Kimberly.

J.L. Hardee

"If you don't come back, I will get custody of our daughter. You're a stripper; they will never give you custody."

Brent Poole pushed his wife into being a stripper, and he was using it against her. These threats did not fall on deaf ears though. Kimberly did not want to lose her only child, and she probably believed that her husband was right. In back woods North Carolina, adultery, stripping, and swinging aren't going to look good on a mother in a custody case. As any mother would, Kimberly did what she had to do to keep her daughter. She broke up with John Boyd Frasier and moved back in with her husband.

What happened next is controversial, and I believe speculation on anyone's part as well. I don't think anyone really knows what happened except Kimberly Renee Poole. This is for sure though. Kimberly Poole planned a vacation for Myrtle Beach, South Carolina to celebrate their 3rd wedding anniversary, and their getting back together. She planned for her family; her husband, daughter, and herself to go to Myrtle Beach for a few days to enjoy some time away from Winston-Salem.

I believe that it was mere speculation on the prosecutor's part, but they told us then that Kimberly Renee Poole conspired at that point with John Boyd Frasier to follow them to Myrtle Beach and to kill her husband. We were told that there would be evidence proving that conspiracy. That the only way John Frasier could have known about their trip was if Kimberly had conspired with him.

Hum? I use to tell my other girlfriends when I would be out of town. That doesn't show a conspiracy to murder anyone. She could have told him she was leaving just so he would know not to try to contact her. There could have been a million reasons why she would have told him. He could have just followed her. He could have done this on his own. He could have been obsessed with her and stalking her. I was already being skeptical, trying to give the defendant the benefit of doubt, waiting for the prosecution to show me the evidence of the conspiracy.

The prosecutor continued with the story without telling us what evidence they would present to show the conspiracy. They told us that on the night of the murder, Kimberly Renee Poole arranged to have a babysitter that worked for the hotel, come to their room for the evening so she could have an evening alone with her husband.

Why do they always use a person's full name when they are charged with murder? I thought.

He told us the two went to dinner and some other places that evening and then returned to the hotel. Kimberly then enticed Brent down to the deserted beach on the premises of having sex. We were told that there was evidence that the two had sex on the beach. There were semen stains in the deceased's underwear and body fluids from both of them on

J.L. Hardee

a towel. What the prosecution told us happened next was based on statements from Kimberly Renee Poole.

Kimberly alleged that after having sex with her husband, someone approached them on the beach. That person wore a mask and demanded money. The alleged robber made Brent Poole get on his knees. William Brent Poole was shot twice, killing him instantly. Either shot would have been enough to have killed him, yet he was shot twice. This was something that was emphasized to show that the intent was to kill Brent Poole, not to rob someone.

They had my attention at this point for sure, because if a robber was going to kill a witness, why not kill both witnesses. A robber would know that the second murder would be a freebie, that the death penalty would be imposed for the first one. *Why wouldn't a robber just kill them both? Why would a robber leave any witnesses to a murder?* The prosecutor pointed out these questions too, but they were running through my mind before he even said anything about it.

He continued with the facts of the case. At some point, Kimberly Renee Poole waved down a Beach Patrol Officer that worked for the City of Myrtle Beach. She had seen headlights coming down the beach, and she ran to the officer screaming for help. She told the officer that her husband had been shot, and they had been robbed. She laid out the story of a lone robber having gunned down her husband. The uniformed patrol officer had no reason to doubt Kimberly Renee Poole's story and they began searching for this masked gunman. No lone gunman was ever found that night.

The prosecutor told us that the police tried to believe Kimberly's story and just took her back to the station for further questioning to get the complete details of what happened. Nothing additional was gained from their questioning of Kimberly that night. However, when they notified Brent Poole's parents of his death, they got their first and only lead in the case that they ever followed.

Brent's parents informed the police of Kimberly's affair with John Boyd Frasier and immediately accused her of the murder. They never believed that it was anyone but Kimberly Renee Poole that murdered their son.

The police jumped right into action. They sent an officer from Winston-Salem Police Department to look for John Boyd Frasier. The murder occurred between 11 p.m. and midnight in Myrtle Beach. If John Boyd Frasier was in Winston-Salem, he couldn't have been the one that did it. When the police in Winston-Salem arrived at the house of John Boyd Frasier between 5-6 a.m. the next morning, they found him at home in bed. They said he appeared to have been sleeping and had been awakened by their visit. The prosecutor told us that the police checked his car, and that it appeared to be cool, as if it hadn't been driven

J.L. Hardee

recently. John Boyd Frasier admitted to a relationship with Kimberly Poole, but denied any knowledge of, or any part in the murder of her husband.

I was puzzled at this point. *Do they believe he did it or not? From what they had said, he was in Winston-Salem and couldn't have done it.* That question in my mind didn't get answered then. They just continued with their story of events.

The prosecutor told us that Kimberly Poole was released and allowed to return to Winston-Salem to bury her husband. Prior to the funeral, the police from Myrtle Beach traveled to Winston-Salem, NC, and they had Kimberly come into the local station there for questioning. Kimberly's family thought she should have an attorney so they contacted their local family attorney; Victor M. Lefkowitz. The prosecution didn't tell us this, but we found it out later that Mr. Lefkowitz was not a criminal defense attorney. He was a family lawyer that specialized in domestic issues. It turned out that he was a quack. With her attorney though, Kimberly voluntarily showed up for questioning.

We were then told that Kimberly Renee Poole gave a complete confession that was taped in which she admitted her involvement in the murder and stated that John Boyd Frasier was the accomplice that committed the act.

Ok. They have a taped confession. This is open and shut. She killed her husband.

I know based on what the judge told us that we were suppose to keep an open mind and listen to both sides, but after the prosecution's opening statement, I was on their side. I was ready to convict right then and there. The prosecution delivered a powerful opening statement and in my mind this was over.

She was guilty.

What could the defense say to counter act the prosecution's opening statement? How are they going to combat a confession? Why are we even here? What is this entire circus about? Let's string her up now and go home. I am sure I wasn't the only one thinking that way after hearing the details of the case that were lined out for us.

CHAPTER IX

The education I received in Loris, SC, had not prepared me for this; not for the real world. There had never been any instructions on the law, court cases, or what we are supposed to do as a juror.

Now, we have cable, internet, crime shows, and forensic shows. A juror stands a little better chance of having some idea of how the system works and what to be prepared for or what to look for.

Back in 1999, when this trial took place, I didn't have Direct TV or anything fancy like that. I had heard of Court TV, but it was not a channel that was offered on my basic cable plan. I had never seen a murder trial on television at that point. I had never seen any forensic crime shows that tell what evidence to look for.

As a graduate of the South Carolina Fire Academy, I received the training and education necessary for my career as a firefighter. Until I began training as an arson investigator after this trial, I had never been instructed on our states laws in a formal fashion.

J.L. Hardee

What my mother and father taught me as to right and wrong was all I had to go on. Can you believe that's what we depend on for children in our society? We hope that their parents taught them right from wrong. Rather than educating our youths on the most important things they're faced with, we worry about whether they know history from 500 years ago or whether they can do advanced calculus. Unless someone is going to be a historian or doctor, we don't need those courses in high school. They are required learning in college anyway. Since the majority of our youths never make it to college, wouldn't it be more prudent to teach them something about life that they will encounter, such as the law.

To this day, I never used algebra or trigonometry since I last took it 15 years ago or longer, but I encountered the law. I am sure that is the case with more people than not. The state criminal procedures manual should be required learning through each year of high school in my opinion.

Since it wasn't when I was taking on my education, I was left with just a simple country mind to judge this case. Some say that this is how it should be. Jurors shouldn't have any sense of the law. I totally disagree with that. Without some formal education on how things work or the law, we are left with having to trust the ones that present the case to you.

J.L. Hardee

I think the case of the Duke Lacrosse prosecutor is evidence enough that we shouldn't just trust the officials that represent a case to us.

In my simple mind, having learned to trust the police and the government, this case was just for show. The prosecutor convinced me with his opening statement.

CHAPTER X

Myrtle Beach Attorney, William Isaac Diggs, had a lot to overcome after the prosecutions opening arguments. His work was going to be cut out for him to even get my attention.

Attorney Diggs was an entirely different character than the soft-spoken professional demeanor of Fran Humphries. Diggs had long, salt and pepper hair which he wore back in a ponytail and a very thick mustache. He didn't look like he was from South Carolina. I was actually curious to see this man in action. I thought he would be some big-time lawyer that would blow this up, maybe.

Diggs' opening statement was surrounded around reasonable doubt and holding the prosecution to their burden of proof. He asked the jury to keep an open mind and make the prosecution show us the proof. It was not the same caliber of performance that the prosecution presented, but he got me to decide to listen further.

Though, after the conclusion of opening arguments, my mind was heavily leaning towards the prosecution, and from that point forward, I

J.L. Hardee

looked for holes in the prosecutions' case to give the defendant the benefit of doubt and to keep an open mind like Attorney Diggs asked. I was already sold at this point. For me, the defense had to show me the holes. They had to show me that there was a lack of evidence.

Even though I was not educated or experienced in these matters, I think I tried to give it my best as a juror. I took very detailed notes from the start to finish. I noted the demeanor and believability of every witness. I noted the evidence that each witness presented.

The prosecution started their case with the beach patrol officer from the City of Myrtle Beach. I remember noting that he presented himself in a very professional manner and that his testimony was believable. Though, his testimony only showed that a crime had been committed. He provided no testimony on who committed the crime. The only notable testimony related to the innocence or guilt of the defendant pertained to her demeanor at the time in question. He testified that the defendant appeared distraught, and genuine in her reactions. There was nothing out of the ordinary about Kimberly Renee Poole in her reactions to the horror that had just taken place.

While I continued to pay close attention and take meticulous notes, the next few witnesses the prosecution presented seemed very minor and immaterial to the case at hand. None of them offered up any real material evidence. The homeowner heard voices. The doctor had a dead

J.L. Hardee

body. Witness after witness and no evidence of who actually committed the crime. I was looking for physical evidence. Where was the gun? Whose finger prints were on it? Who owned the gun? Where were the ballistics experts? I didn't even know what that was at the time, but I was expecting something with some concrete evidence. They were asking us to convict someone of murder.

There were 9mm bullets found at the scene. I thought that the prosecution would be presenting some evidence as to where they came from or who the owner was. Were there any fingerprints on them or DNA evidence? I didn't even know what DNA evidence was back then, but there wasn't any presented.

There were 3 big witnesses for the prosecution. They were the two detectives who investigated the case and obtained the alleged confession and the eye witnesses that supposedly identified John Boyd Frasier.

The first of those three that was brought to testify was Detective John King. Detective King worked for the City of Myrtle Beach Police. He was a very well dressed man with a tight hair cut and a professional demeanor. I remember thinking that he looked more like a celebrity rather than a police detective.

My curiosity was pegged when Detective King took the stand. I was hoping for someone to finally present some evidence that backed up the prosecutor's statement. I was looking for someone to back up my initial

J.L. Hardee

conclusions that this was an open-and-shut case. Finally, there was a witness that was going to put the nail in the coffin.

Detective King walked us through the case and presented us with the taped confessions. After listening to the tapes, and the testimony of Detective King on direct examination by the prosecutor, it was a rap for me. This well-dressed, soft-spoken, little man wasn't intimidating enough to coerce a confession. I was locked in with the prosecution at this point. After hours of listening to tapes, my mind was starting to wonder. I still tried to pay attention, but it was getting boring and redundant. Up to this point, the prosecution showed me all I needed to see. I was just waiting for the end. Let's get done with this already.

That day of testimony ended with the testimony of Detective King, and I went to sleep that night thinking that Kimberly Renee Poole was definitely guilty. The Defense decided to hold their cross for the next morning.

In hind sight, I don't think that was a good move on the defense's part. I am sure the entire jury felt the same that night. We were all left to sleep on the impression that this girl confessed and it wasn't rebutted.

The following day, defense attorney Diggs began his questioning of Detective King, and he did so with a vengeance. He laid into that detective. It was the kind of questioning that you would expect from a seasoned defense attorney.

J.L. Hardee

I can't recall all of the testimony of Detective King during his cross-examination, but the most important part of his testimony turned out to be one little statement that turned things on its head. It had nothing to do with the taped confession. It had nothing to do with his competency or the evidence that he gathered. It didn't matter how well-dressed he was.

Attorney Diggs asked the Detective at which point he considered the defendant a suspect. He was trying to inquire as to why the detective had not read the defendant her Miranda rights. In a series of questions strategically put forth by Diggs, he laid a trap for the soft-spoken detective. We could tell the detective was getting flustered with the defense attorney, but it finally had me interested in this case again.

Detective John King testified under oath before us, the jury, that he did not consider Kimberly Renee Poole a suspect prior to her interview, questioning, or interrogation. He informed us that he only considered the defendant a suspect after she confessed.

WOW! That's all I can remember thinking at this point.

Why would he say that? I couldn't understand it. Of course he had to have considered her a suspect. Anyone would have considered her a suspect just because she was the wife, and after having received information from Brent's family regarding the affair and information about John Boyd Frasier, any detective with more than a day of experience would consider Renee a suspect. If that's so, then why would

J.L. Hardee

he tell us that he didn't consider her a suspect? I was astonished. This detective had just lied to us under oath in a court of law. Why did he do that though? It took me a little while to figure out that answer. I remember my notes and taking them on that day. I specifically noted in bold, *Detective John King of the Myrtle Beach Police Department lied on witness stand.* The detective lied about considering the defendant a suspect in order to get her taped confession into evidence, because her Miranda rights had obviously been violated.

I really didn't care about the defendant's Miranda rights. They didn't mean a thing to me. I would have convicted her regardless of her rights. What did matter to me was that I was supposed to place my faith in evidence that was collected by someone that just lied to me.

I remember my next statement in my notes, *don't place any weight on the testimony of Detective John King, because he lied to me under oath.*

The defense finally got my attention and made me reawaken. I was going to start paying close attention to this case and I know prosecution witnesses are willing to lie to convict this defendant.

I was actually waiting for the judge to step in and do something about the detective having lied. *Why isn't Judge Cottingham doing something about this?* I thought there should've been a mistrial right then.

JUSTICE OR INJUSTICE?

Why are we still here? The prosecutions' chief witness is a liar. I could care less that he lied to the defendant to obtain her confession. What I did care about was that he lied to me for no reason. I couldn't get that out of my mind.

The prosecutor obviously didn't care that a prime witness and lead detective in his case lied, because he just continued with the next witness. That made me lose a little respect for the man I had started to admire, Fran Humphries.

Detective Terry Altman was up next. He was really the prosecutions primary witness in this case. I was hoping from the start that Detective Altman would do something to fix the mess that Detective King left. I wanted to stay on the side of the prosecution, especially if she had really done this, and I was hoping that Detective Altman would have something solid to make me ignore his colleague.

Just like Detective King before him, Terry Altman put on a stellar performance walking us through the case and the tapes of the interrogation. After his direct testimony, he had me back on track. Detective Altman appeared to be your average country boy like me. He wore a suit and presented a well-dressed, professional manner, but he wasn't wearing duds like John King. He just looked normal to me. That allowed me to follow him and believe what he was telling me. I was able to see it just as he said it was. This defendant was guilty. She confessed

J.L. Hardee

and he had it on tape. He showed a pattern of inconsistencies with her statements and really left me with no doubt of her guilt. Okay, this case was over with again. The prosecution had made up for Detective King's deception.

How could the defense counter this?

Defense Attorney Diggs began questioning Detective Altman with a little more finesse than the previous witness. He started out talking softly and just asking simple questions. He asked the detective about his training and experience and pointed out that he had only been a detective for two years.

I remember thinking, *no big deal*. I was starting to lose interest again with the case and this line of questioning. My mind was wondering to my wife and kids and getting home.

Then Diggs proposed the same question to Altman that King had lied about and I remember sitting back up and staring at him for his response. Detective Terry Altman said that on the night in question he never considered the defendant a suspect. He admitted having heard from the victim's family and them accusing her and John Boyd Frasier. He told us that he just considered her to be a witness to the crime and that it didn't warrant Miranda warnings.

There it goes again. Another Myrtle Beach Police Detective just lied to me, to the jury, in a capital murder trial.

This man does not appear to be that dumb. He had to have considered her a suspect. I don't know the law, but I assume that both of the detectives had to lie about when they considered the defendant a suspect in order to get her taped confession admitted into evidence.

All that mattered to me was two detectives, sworn to uphold the law, and persons that are to be an example for others to follow, lied to us under oath. I remember the clerk's statement, "do you swear to tell the truth, the whole truth, and nothing but the truth, so help you God?" Both of them had sworn that they would provide the whole truth and they hadn't.

My trust in the State, in the Prosecution's office, and the police was just diminished. It was bad enough that one detective tried to deceive the jury, but two detectives did it.

If they will lie to me about this, then what else are they lying about? If the prosecutor will allow them to lie to us, then what else is the prosecutor willing to do? I just lost all faith in the people that I had looked up to.

CHAPTER XI

After the testimony of the two lead detectives, I was left very confused and unsure of what to think. I didn't know what to do. I have to admit that after that, I didn't pay as close attention to the case. I continued taking notes and listening, but my mind was wandering. I just kept hoping that there would be some stronger, more credible witnesses.

The prosecution continued with their case without any delays. Witness after witness laid out their case just as the prosecutor said it would be in his opening statement. I just kept looking for the smoking gun that was going to turn this back around for me.

When the prosecutor called the eye witness to the stand, I decided to redirect my mind to that testimony. I was expecting this person to be a strong witness for the prosecution. The witness supposedly had positively identified John Boyd Frasier as the trigger man in this case.

There were actually two eye witnesses and they were a married couple that was also vacationing in Myrtle Beach. They had no axe to grind in this case. They appeared to be very respectable, middle-aged people. I listened to their testimony intently.

The prosecution walked us through the night of events from the witness' point of view. They had been walking along the beach between eleven and midnight and they saw a guy dressed in black that looked out of place. His demeanor didn't look right, so they decided to leave the area. They hadn't witnessed the crime. They just saw someone that looked out of place prior to the events that transpired that evening. Both of the witnesses gave different accounts of what happened and how the perpetrator looked. However, both positively identified John Boyd Frasier from a police photo lineup a few days after the incident.

I was really confused. My mind was really racing. The two witnesses appeared credible. They appeared to be nice people. They told me they were sure that John Boyd Frasier was the guy. Then I remembered that two detectives lied to me in this case and the police were also involved in the lineup.

Did the police do something to suggest who the culprit was? Before, that question wouldn't have entered my mind, but after two witnesses had lied, I had to question what I was hearing.

I began to play out the scenario in my head with the help of questions from Attorney Diggs. These two witnesses were on a dark beach, around midnight, in questionable lighting, and a few days later were able to positively, 100% identify the person they saw that night for just a brief moment.... I just couldn't believe it. I know those two witnesses meant well and weren't purposely lying like the two detectives did, but I just couldn't believe what they were telling me. The defense attorney definitely put upon reasonable doubt in my mind with those two witnesses.

After that, I hoped the prosecution had something else for me to hang my hat on, but it never came. The prosecution rested their case after a few days of testimony without ever fixing the damage from the two detectives.

CHAPTER XII

For me this case was over. The prosecution had rested. There would be no more evidence presented against this defendant. What began for me as an open-and-shut case for the prosecution came to a close with a definite win for the defense.

I don't even remember the defense's witnesses. I listened to them, and I was present when they testified, but I didn't even take notes during the defense's case. I was hoping to hear from Kimberly Renee Poole, but it really didn't matter to me. My mind was made up. The judge told us that the prosecution had the burden to prove the defendant's guilt, and the defense was not responsible for proving her innocence.

If I could have placed faith in the testimony of the two lead detective's my decision would have be different. To me, the eye-witnesses weren't that strong. The only strong evidence the prosecution had was a taped confession that was obtained and presented into

J.L. Hardee

evidence by two detectives that lied. Why should I put any weight on their testimony? I couldn't. No matter how much we want to seek the truth or to seek justice or to do what is right or if we feel she may have been guilty, we can't base our decision off of a lie. I had a real moral dilemma. In my heart, I felt that Kimberly Renee Poole may have had something to do with this. I still had reservations about that though. They never even proved that John Boyd Frasier was the trigger man. They surely hadn't proved that Kimberly conspired with him. Even if he was the one that did it, it didn't mean she conspired with him. He could have done it all alone in a jealous rage. He could have just followed her to the beach and shot Brent Poole after he saw them having sex. All she confessed was telling Frazier where she would be and admitting that he 'could have been the person that shot her husband'.

All of these thoughts ran through my head. *Detectives John King and Terry Altman lied, under oath, in a court of law. Why should I, or anyone, believe anything they say?* I was really confused. I didn't know what to do. I remember having a real tough time sleeping the night before the final day. The two detectives put me into a tough spot. The theory of the prosecution's case was very plausible, but I had to base my decision on evidence and the lack of evidence.

Kimberly Renee Poole never took the stand in her defense and the prosecutor wasn't able to discuss her alleged confession or try to combat the perjured testimony of the two detectives. Without getting her tripped up on the witness stand, and being able to get her to admit guilt in this case, the prosecutor had sealed this case himself.

There was not one piece of physical evidence in this case that could prove anyone had done this. There weren't any fingerprints or DNA. They never found the weapon and were never able to tie a gun to Kimberly Renee Poole or John Boyd Frazier. There wasn't any blood evidence. They didn't find any bloody or conspicuous clothes on John Boyd Frazier. The only physical evidence in the case was a beach towel, and the deceased's underwear with semen stains. The only thing that proved was two married people had sex on the beach. If anything, that helped the defense. If she really conspired, and participated with John Boyd Frazier to have her husband killed, are we to think they would agree she would have sex with her husband one last time? My thinking was just the opposite. If she had really planned this and conspired with Frazier, the murder would've taken place before the sex.

Without any physical evidence, I hoped there would be some strong witnesses, but there wasn't. There weren't any credible witnesses. This was nothing but a circumstantial case, and one that should have never made it to trial.

J.L. Hardee

I dressed in my best clothes on the final day. I saved them for the end. We all knew that this case was coming to a close. The two parties rested their cases and we were going to return the following day for closing arguments and jury instructions.

CHAPTER XIII

The final day came and the time was near. We spent the last part of the morning listening to instructions from the judge. The attorneys gave closing arguments, but I don't recall paying much attention to them. Closing arguments wasn't evidence, and this case was over. All of the evidence had been presented. I spent the night tossing and turning, making up my mind what I would do that final day.

After the Honorable Edward Cottingham gave his closing remarks, we were able to take a break. I went to smoke a cigarette, and we were allowed to eat lunch. The Jury in the case of the State of SC vs. Kimberly Renee Poole began its deliberations shortly after noon on that final day. We were left with a great responsibility of deciding the fate of someone's life.

I won't ever forget that day. Some aspects of the case are a little fuzzy after all of these years, but that one day rests in my head like a thorn in my side.

J.L. Hardee

This is when this story really begins....

Everything that happened prior to this was just foreplay. The real drama lies in the Jury Room. I didn't know that at the time. I also didn't know that I had just smoked my last cigarette and was in for some real work.

When I entered the Jury Room for deliberations, I had no idea how we were supposed to do things. I knew what my decision was, but I didn't know how things would proceed. Everyone was surprisingly very calm. We ate lunch just prior to our deliberations, and we were all full and ready to go home. The end was near. We should be out of here in an hour I thought. I was going to get to see my son soon. I was going to get to go home and make love to my wife.

That's what I was thinking about. Not about the case. The case was over and I was sure we were done.

I remember asking, "How are we going to do this?"

The Jury Foreperson was Gail Whitehead. She appeared to be in her late forties or early fifties with a short boy cut hairstyle. I hadn't spoken with Mrs. Whitehead much if any prior to this day. She just didn't seem approachable, and I wasn't paying her much attention. That would change on this day.

Mrs. Whitehead took charge immediately like a drill instructor from Paris Island. She said, "I think we should just go ahead and vote and see if we can get out of here."

I was right on with that. "Let's do it." I said.

She continued by asking how we would like to vote. Would we like to all raise our hands, or would we all like to do it by secret ballot? I was all about being quick and just raising our hands. However, this quiet, little old lady spoke up and said she preferred to use secret ballots. That was it.

Mrs. Whitehead said, "We'll all do secret ballots." She continued by instructing us to write our verdicts on a piece of paper and to write the verdict next to each charge and to fold it up and pass it forward when we were done. She explained that she would read the verdicts after viewing them.

The judge never instructed us to any specific rules as how this was supposed to be done. When Gail Whitehead took the lead and gave instructions, we all followed her. One may think that this would be a process that took several minutes, but it didn't. It was really quick. We all wrote down our verdicts and just as quickly as we began, it was over. We passed the folded slips of paper up to the front of the table.

A look of frustration passed over Gail Whitehead's face. After looking at the verdicts she said, "It doesn't look like we'll be getting out of here any time soon, we're split."

We all thought we would be done in fifteen minutes or less and we were wrong. I learned something that day. If a jury isn't done in less than half an hour, they are hung. Juries don't want to be there any longer than they have to be. They don't have to really review the evidence again. Everyone had walked into that room, at the conclusion of the case, with their minds made up one way or the other.

There were 6 votes for guilty on both charges of murder and conspiracy to commit murder. There were 4 votes for not guilty on both charges and there were two split votes. The two split votes were guilty for conspiracy, but not guilty on the murder.

Gail then said, "secret ballots aren't going to work. We need to all state our verdicts out loud."

Objections were raised by some, especially the little old lady. Those objections fell on deaf ears though. I didn't really care about that. I wasn't ashamed of my verdict, and whatever we needed to do to speed this process up would be great for me.

We were only 15 minutes into our deliberations and we were a hung jury!

J.L. Hardee

Gail Whitehead took charge though. She went around the table, starting with the gentleman to her right. I was wondering why she didn't just announce her own verdict first. Maybe she wanted to see what the others would do before sharing her own personal thoughts.

The gentleman on the right loudly said, "I think she's guilty, on both charges!"

Without any discussion as to our reasons for coming to our verdicts, Gail continued around the room, gathering each Juror's verdict.

This jury was pretty evenly split between men and women. I don't recall the exact makeup, but I remember that it was pretty equal.

Most of the men had voted guilty. One man was a split juror.

When it came my turn to announce my verdict, I did so with conviction in my voice. "My vote is not guilty on both charges."

I was the only man voting 'not guilty' on both counts. As Gail continued around the room, most of the women voted 'not guilty'. One woman was the other split juror.

I could see that this was going to take a long time already.

After we all stated our verdicts, Gail asked, "Is everyone sure about their verdict?"

Everyone agreed that they were confident in their decision. Gail decided to send a note out to the judge. We had been in there less than an hour when Gail Whitehead knocked on the door.

J.L. Hardee

The bailiff entered the room. Mrs. Whitehead handed him a note for the judge.

Ok, we're done. That was simple. We will be out of here soon. She told the judge we were hung. Obviously, the judge wasn't right on the other side of the door. I don't know what happened outside of that room, but it took a little while before the bailiff returned. We just sat there chilling. I was getting ready to leave. My job was done. I heard the evidence and I gave my vote.

J.L. Hardee

CHAPTER XIV

I never learned what happened when we submitted the note to the judge telling him that we were hung. Did the bailiff just take it to him in chambers? Was it presented in open court in front of the attorneys? I still don't know.

What I do recall is, when the bailiff walked back in, he simply said, "the judge said to continue deliberating. You haven't spent enough time on this."

What? I didn't have the guts to say that aloud, but I wish I had.

Was there new evidence? Was there something else?

We heard the evidence. We, in good conscious, made a decision, and we voted with our beliefs based on the evidence that had been presented. That is something that everyone should remember....

The Jury voted our true verdict and sent it out in less than an hour. We were hung.

J.L. Hardee

I was frustrated. I asked the bailiff for a break. I wanted to go smoke a cigarette. The bailiff said he would ask the judge. I was at the door waiting for the bailiff with cigarettes in hand.

Want to talk about frustration? My frustration turned to anger when the bailiff returned. The judge said that the jury can't take breaks during deliberations. You will have to continue until you reach a verdict.

I was pissed!

We all just sat there for a few moments not really knowing what to do next. They didn't teach us in school how to be a juror, and they surely hadn't told us during the trial or jury instructions what to do if we were hung.

Our only instructions were to continue deliberating.

Are we supposed to manufacture a verdict? Why didn't they just tell us how they wanted us to vote if they weren't going to use our true verdict?

Gail Whitehead broke the silence and said, "We need to discuss the case and determine how we all came to our verdicts." She looked to the juror on her right. He was a middle-aged gentleman that didn't speak much.

She didn't have to say anything to him. I guess he understood from her look what she wanted from him.

J.L. Hardee

He began by saying, "It's simple for me. She confessed. They have it on tape. My vote is guilty."

Gail Whitehead asked, "Is there anything else that made you choose that verdict?"

"I am sure there's more, but it was mostly because of the taped confession." He replied.

The next juror was a young man probably just a few years older than me. He said, "Who else would have done it? I would have believed it was her even if she hadn't confessed. The confession was just icing on the cake for me."

Hum?

That wasn't something I agreed with. How were we supposed to get someone that thinks like that to see reasoning?

We had not even pulled out one piece of evidence. All of the physical evidence, such as diagrams, police reports, and so forth were lined up in the corner of the room for us to assist in our deliberations.

Not one person thought about going back over the evidence at this point.

One by one, everyone gave their brief explanation as to why they reached the verdict they did. When they reached the fourth gentleman, he explained that he thought she conspired with John Boyd Frasier by telling him where they would be, but he disagreed with her being found guilty of murder, because even the prosecution said she didn't pull the trigger.

One of the female jurors spoke up. "That's what I think, too."

Those two jurors had an issue with the law. They said that they were willing to find her guilty of conspiracy, but were definitely not going to vote guilty on murder.

I began thinking that may be a compromise I would be willing to make to speed this up and get out of here, but I never said anything about it.

The table we were all seated at was a long rectangular table with chairs on each end and several in the middle. I was seated at the end of the table on the far end of the room. On the opposite end of the table, Jury Foreperson Gail Whitehead was at the throne.

To my left, all of the men were seated beside each other, and to my right, all of the women were seated. We were all separated and divided right down the middle of that table.

One would think that this process would go quickly, but it seemed to be very slow.

Eventually they got to me. I was the first outright 'not guilty' vote. I decided to give a little more explanation to my verdict than just a simple sentence. I told them all that to begin with, from the start of the prosecution's opening statement, I pretty much made up my mind that she was guilty.

"Well, what changed your mind?" Gail Whitehead interrupted before I could even continue explaining.

I pulled out my yellow notepad. I flipped through the pages until I got to the testimony of Detective John King. "Do you remember Detective King's testimony?" I asked. Some said yeah, and some just shook their heads in agreement.

I started walking them through Detective King's testimony. I took meticulous notes. I pointed out all of his good points first. Then, I pointed out he was the one that presented the taped confession.

"Well, what was wrong with his testimony?" Gail Whitehead interrupted me again.

I was fully planning on getting to that before she rudely interrupted me. I was starting to get frustrated with her. My earlier and continued frustration up to this point was with the judge for making us continue with our deliberations after we made a decision. I was really angry because I wasn't allowed to take a smoke break and now I have someone interrupting me every time I speak.

"The simple answer was because he lied." I stated.

"When did he lie?" Gail yelled.

This was going to be a debate between Gail and me, I could see. I read to her word for word the question that was asked of him and his response. "It's very obvious that he lied. He had to have considered her a suspect from the beginning." I stated.

The little old black lady chimed in and said that she agreed, and so did the other jurors that voted not guilty. They came to my rescue. The only reason I pointed out that the little old woman was black is because Detective King is a black male as well. I didn't want to seem as a racist or anything. That had nothing to do with my views, and I was glad to see that a black woman agreed with me.

"Well, what does that have to do with anything?" Gail demanded. "She confessed! So what if he did? Does that mean we should ignore her confession?"

"Yes, it does. If he is going to lie to us about one thing, how can we believe anything else he says?"

Gail continued, "We have the right to believe all, none, or part of a witness' testimony."

"You are right! I choose not to believe anything said before or after he lied to me."

"Me either!" Another juror stated.

We hadn't even gotten to Detective Altman's perjured testimony. We argued about Detective King for a while. None of us debated if

Detective King lied. We all agreed on that point. The only debate was whether his lie mattered. The only thing this jury could agree on was a Myrtle Beach police detective lied under oath in a murder trial.

Most of the men that had voted guilty just sat quietly. Gail was the only 'guilty' vote that was speaking. She really took her role as Jury Foreperson to heart.

Gail finally said, "We are getting nowhere like this. Let's continue."

Around the table we continued. The nice little old lady was sitting directly to my right. She was up next. "They just didn't prove it to me. There wasn't any evidence. I don't believe her confession, not after 17 hours of interrogation and they didn't show me anything else."

Up next was a middle-aged country girl that looked like she grew up in Aynor. That's more backwoods than Loris, where I was raised. She spoke very softly. "I just don't believe the police. I believe that a few of them lied to us. I'm not sure what to believe after that. I am sure that Detective King lied like he said." She looked at me.

The next person to speak was the woman that had a split vote. She said, "You already know how I feel. I will vote guilty for conspiracy, but not for murder. She is definitely not the one that killed her husband. Someone else did. I am not sending someone to prison forever if they weren't the one that did it."

Why doesn't Gail interrupt them and chime in with her opinion about their verdict? I thought.

The next juror was another definite 'not guilty'. She said, "That black detective and the white one both lied to us. I can't remember their names, but they lied to us," she continued.

I began thinking to myself. *If those two detectives hadn't lied we would already have been out of here. We would probably only have the two split jurors to deal with. The rest of us may have voted 'guilty'. We are stuck in this jury room, without a cigarette, because two Myrtle Beach detectives thought we were too dumb to recognize that they lied to us.*

Gail Whitehead was the last to speak. She began by saying that she agreed with us. "The two detectives lied and that may be perjury, but that was for the judge to deal with, not for us. We can believe the rest of their testimony and I do," she proclaimed. "They have her confession on tape and I believe that she's guilty."

It appeared that Gail must have some experience with this. She seemed like she may have done this before. She definitely acted like she had some education regarding the law. "Are any of you willing to change your votes?" She asked.

"NO!"

J.L. Hardee

Everyone was pretty adamant about that. Nobody was willing to change their decision.

We, the jury, had voted and discussed our true beliefs in our verdicts. We went around the entire table and each person was able to express their views and reasons for their vote.

"Well, I will send another note to the judge."

I have no idea what Gail wrote on her notes to the judge. All I know is that she sent a slip of paper out to the bailiff to give to the judge.

It was about 2:30 or 3 p.m. when the second note was sent out to the judge. It should have said, "WE'RE DONE", "WE'RE HOPELESSLY HUNG." I doubt she put it like that.

A few minutes after she handed out the note, I began pacing. There wasn't even room for me to do that, but I was wiggling around the best I could. I was ready to go home. I was definitely ready to be out of that small room we were crammed in. I needed a cigarette. I needed some fresh air. I was ready to relax, and I couldn't relax in that jury room.

CHAPTER XV

I wondered what was going on in the courtroom. *What are they doing? When are they coming to get us?* I wasn't worried about that as much as I was just having a break to myself, but it was on my mind.

Again, I was by the door when the bailiff knocked. When he opened up, he slipped a note back to Gail. The judge sent a reply. I thought we should have all been entitled to see that note, but we weren't.

Gail said, "We have to continue deliberating until we reach a verdict. We haven't had enough time to go over the evidence."

Did the judge tell her we can't leave until we reach a verdict that he agrees with? Why didn't we get to see that note? What verdict does he want? What are we supposed to do? What were his instructions? Did he say we were going to be stuck here for life if we didn't find her guilty?

"Hold up! I need a break. We can continue, but I want a break first." I knocked on the door. Politely as I could be, I asked the bailiff for a smoke break. He told me that the judge wouldn't allow it. I insisted that he go ask again. I don't even know if he relayed my request to the judge.

J.L. Hardee

We can't see what goes on outside of the jury room. I just hoped that my requests were really being considered.

I was ignoring the rest of the room. They weren't really doing anything though. Some of them were chatting about their personal lives. I think we were all done with the case at that point, in our minds at least.

The bailiff returned and said, "There would be no breaks allowed outside of the jury room, but the judge has agreed to let you open a window and smoke in here if none of the other jurors have a problem with it."

"Cool!" I began to pull my cigs out. I had one in my mouth ready to light it and guess who spoke up.

The Honorable Gail Whitehead said, "I don't like secondhand smoke."

You want to talk about pissed. I was ready to open the window and throw her out with that remark. I had been asking for a cigarette break for nearly 2 hours and the judge finally agreed, but only if the other jurors did.

No such luck. I wouldn't be allowed to smoke in the room. Gail addressed her complaints about that to the bailiff, and he told me I couldn't smoke.

One may not agree with my reactions. One may not agree with my verdict. One may not agree with how I arrived at my verdict, but this we should all agree on.

A juror should not be forced to decide someone's fate while they are angry. A juror shouldn't be forced to a decision under any additional stress. All I wanted was a break. We took two votes. Well, one vote and one full explanation of our vote and we all had decided that we were hung. Our minds were made up. In my mind, my job was done. I did what was asked of me. I was asked to hear the evidence presented to me and to make a vote. I made my vote. The judge had our vote. *What do we do now? What is the point?* I was mad. *There's no way I'm changing my vote.*

Before someone throws darts at me, I wasn't the only smoker in that room. I wasn't the only one upset with being forced to continue our deliberations. I surely wasn't the only one that wanted a break. I was just the only one complaining about it. I really didn't complain that much though. I kept most of my thoughts to myself. Anyone with any sense could see my frustration though.

We all just sat there for a few moments, collected our thoughts and tried to calm down. Gail took it upon herself to finally pull out some evidence. She began discussing the case and discussing the evidence. I must admit that I wasn't paying much attention. I listened to her though,

J.L. Hardee

as she tried to convince the other women that they should change their votes.

"It appears that the only way we're getting out of here is if we reach a unanimous verdict." Gail stated.

I agreed with her on that point. That was made obviously clear to us. She didn't even bother talking to the men that were sided with her 'guilty' vote. She started talking to the lady next to her. She was a definite 'not guilty' on both charges. I couldn't even hear everything that Gail was saying to her. Some of the others were talking amongst themselves and it had nothing to do with the case. For all I knew, Gail offered to buy the woman a steak if she changed her verdict.

I do remember Gail speaking up at one point and saying that there was no way to combat her confession. "Kimberly Renee Poole confessed and it was all on tape. We can't just ignore her confession. None of the other evidence even matters. She confessed!"

I had to interrupt her. I couldn't help it. I had been polite all I could. If it was ok for her to interrupt me, then I was going to do the same.

"The only way you can believe her confession is if you believe the people that took her confession!" I stated loudly. "Since we can't believe the two detectives that took her confession, then we can't believe the confession itself. Besides, they interrogated this girl for 17 hours straight. I have been in this room with you for about 3 hours now and

I'm ready to tell you anything you want to hear, so I can get out of here. I'm sure Kimberly Renee Poole felt the same way. How can we believe anything she said on those tapes after 17 hours?"

I was willing to confess to the JFK assignation if it meant we could get out of there and I wasn't even born yet when he died.

I continued, "If the detectives hadn't lied then I'd probably feel differently, but they did, and I can't, in good conscious, rely on any of their testimony. If there had been other evidence showing her guilt, then I could reconsider, but there wasn't any other evidence. Is there anything that corroborates the alleged confession?"

"What about the two eye witnesses?" One of the male jurors stated.

"What? The eyewitnesses?"

"Yeah, the eyewitnesses that saw John Boyd Frasier."

"Well, to begin with, I didn't believe them either, but even if I did believe them; even if I believed that John Boyd Frasier was the trigger man, that doesn't mean that Mrs. Poole conspired with him. He could've easily found out where she was going and followed them here."

"That's not likely." He said. "That's not reasonable. Who else would have done it if it wasn't John Frasier?"

"I don't know. I don't know that he did it, but for argument sake, let's say he did. Does that fact in itself prove the Kimberly was involved? Does that prove that she conspired with him?"

J.L. Hardee

Gail couldn't help herself. "We have her on tape saying that she did."

"I've already explained to you my reasoning with those tapes and with the detectives that recorded them. Those tapes are useless to me."

The gentleman continued. "I agree that the detectives over embellished and probably told a little white one, but that doesn't mean that we have to ignore the rest of their testimony or the interrogation."

"I disagree."

"Look, this girl is a stripper who cheated on her husband, she doesn't deserve our sympathy." Can you guess who made that statement? I will let your imagination wander.

"Oh, just because she was a stripper and she cheated, that means we should convict her of murder?" I didn't get an answer to that question from the person it was directed at.

The gentleman, who had been speaking replied though. "I could care less that she was a stripper. I don't see how she was. She isn't that attractive, but that doesn't matter to me, and I really don't care who she slept with. We have her confession on tape."

"This girl slept with ten different men, and women too while she was married." Gail chimed in. "Her boyfriend killed her husband and she planned it with him. I think she is guilty and I am not changing my mind on that. The rest of you can say what you want, but I'm not going to vote 'not guilty' for this girl."

J.L. Hardee

Does it matter that she was a stripper? Does it matter if she had an affair? Does that make her a murderer? I thought.

This was getting personal and heated. It was turning away from the facts of the case and was now about her profession and her sex life.

I had to respond. "Does it mean that she conspired with him just because she cheated?"

I told the jurors a bit about me that I hoped to keep private. "My wife cheated on me and after she did, I went out and got another woman for myself. Neither one of us conspired to kill each other over it. Cheating doesn't make someone guilty of murder."

"How else would he have known where they were and when?" Gail replied.

Since Gail was obviously naïve when it came to matters like this, I decided to explain some more to her.

"Gail, I had a girlfriend for a little bit while I was married. I used to tell her everywhere I went. She knew exactly when I was going out of town and where I would be and when I'd be returning. I made her aware of this so she wouldn't call continuously and make my wife suspicious."

"Maybe Kimberly told John Boyd Frasier that she would be out of town. Maybe she was still seeing him. That doesn't mean that she conspired with him. Maybe John got jealous when Kimberly moved out and decided to follow her to the beach. These are a lot of maybes', and I

J.L. Hardee

personally can't make decisions that will affect the rest of someone's life on a 'maybe'. The fact is that there just isn't enough evidence in this case."

"What about the confession?" She kept coming back to that confession.

I can't remember the exact details of the taped interrogations. They were more than 17 hours long. I remember telling Gail though, "All she confessed was telling her boyfriend she would be going out of town, and she said that after the cops threatened to take her daughter away from her."

I could see that this was going to be an ongoing debate between Gail and me. I really didn't feel like explaining myself anymore. The other jurors had just been sitting silently while Gail and I went back and forth. I decided to stop talking. I wasn't getting anywhere. Whether I was right or wrong, I tried to explain my views and how I came to my verdict. It just wasn't getting through, and I was tired of trying.

CHAPTER XVI

The other jurors had the same looks of frustration that I felt. It was about 4 p.m. We had been in that room since noon. We had lunch first and probably didn't do our first vote until 1 p.m., but we had been in this tiny room for nearly 4 hours.

What should I do in this situation? What can I do? I had no idea. I didn't even care anymore. I wanted to do what I believed was right, but not at the cost of my sanity.

One of the male jurors asked if he could speak. He said that he would like to understand why the two jurors with a split vote made that conclusion. Both of them spoke up immediately. They seemed pretty strong with their beliefs. They both had the same reasoning. They didn't believe she should be found guilty of murder if she wasn't the one that pulled the trigger.

Gail Whitehead took it upon herself to single these two jurors out then. She was finally off of my back.

J.L. Hardee

She explained, "The law says that she's just as guilty as the one that did it." I knew Gail was right about that one, but that wasn't my position, and I surely didn't agree with her out loud. Gail began explaining the law to these two Jurors as if she was a law school graduate. She pushed them. "Do you believe she conspired with John Frasier to kill Brent Poole? You voted guilty on conspiracy so you must believe she conspired with him."

"Yes." They both answered.

"If you believe that then, you have to vote 'guilty' on both charges. She can't be guilty of one and not the other."

Since when is Gail the scholar of law and the one that is supposed to tell us how to follow the law? Isn't that the Judge's job?

I wanted to butt in and say, *she's not guilty on both*, but I kept my mouth shut. I agreed with everything Gail was saying about the law, as I knew it, even though I didn't think it was her place to be instructing on it. I just didn't believe there was enough evidence to find guilt on either charge under the law.

It wasn't a matter of whether or not she actually did it in my mind. It was a matter of point and principle that the prosecution failed to prove it to me conclusively. I wasn't willing to send someone to jail unless I was absolutely sure of their guilt.

J.L. Hardee

Gail continued debating with the two jurors for about half an hour while the rest of us just sat and listened in silence. I don't know if any of the other jurors were even paying attention to the debate in front of them.

At about 4:30 p.m. that afternoon, our jury foreperson took it upon herself to send out a note to the judge. She didn't even consult the rest of the jurors. I had no idea what was in this note. One would think that the rest of the jurors would be entitled to that information, but we were just left guessing.

I looked at the lady to my right and just shook my head as I thought. *What is Gail doing? What did she write on that note? Is she God in here? Did she finally ask for a break? Why didn't she ask us before she sent out a note? Does she know the judge or something? Are they passing notes in study-hall? Is she allowed to have private conversations with the judge that we don't know about?* Gail and the Judge exchanging private notes with each other during jury deliberations really disturbed me.

About 10 minutes later, the bailiff showed up at the door. I was excited. Finally, I thought, *we are going to get a break.*

He asked for all of the jurors to come into the court room.

Ok! This is over with. This isn't a break. We are done. The judge finally accepted that we are hung. I was relieved. It was a complete

J.L. Hardee

weight lifted off of my shoulders. We were going home soon. Someone else would have to hash out this case.

The case of the State of SC vs. Kimberly Renee Poole was over. It ended in a hung jury.

CHAPTER XVII

The jurors were all directed to the jury box. One would think that I would have been near the front, with the anticipation of getting out of there. I wasn't though. I hadn't known about this. Whatever Gail Whitehead did, she did it without telling the rest of us. If she did tell anyone, I didn't hear her, and I know several of the others didn't either because they thought we were going home, too.

As we sat down in the box, the judge took the bench. "The Jury Foreperson has sent out a note asking for clarification on the law. Unless there are any objections, I'm going to charge the jury with the law as related to this case."

The judge read the law out loud to us. He instructed us on the law as it pertained to circumstantial evidence and the law of conspiracy. "The hand of one is the hand of all," I remember him saying.

I know what Gail did. She got tired of arguing with those two jurors and took it upon herself to get some backup.

Shouldn't the rest of the Jurors have been included in that decision? Is the foreperson of a jury God? Is the foreperson like the judge? My thoughts were all over the place.

The judge handed us down a copy of the law in which he had just read from and directed us back to our deliberations.

I was really frustrated then.

I am ready to go, I kept thinking. *How much longer is this going to go on?*

When we sat back down in the jury room, Gail immediately said, "See? I was right. If you think she's guilty of conspiracy then she's guilty of murder too. Can we take another vote?"

The gentleman to her right, a 'guilty vote' said, "Let's just take another vote and see where we are."

Not a single person in that room even laid out any discussion about what just happened or about their positions related to what we heard.

Around the table we went. None of the other jurors got to express their opinions. They just started voting out loud again.

No problem for me. I wasn't ashamed of my decision.

"Guilty!"

"Guilty!"

"Guilty!"

"Guilty!"

J.L. Hardee

"Guilty!"

Oops, the man that was split changed his vote. I was up next.

"Not Guilty!"

"Not Guilty!"

"Guilty!"

"Not Guilty!"

"Guilty!"

"Not Guilty!"

"Guilty!"

The woman changed her split vote too. It was 8-4. We were still split though. It was about 5 p.m. or so at this point. At this point, we had been in that jury room for 5 hours. The jury foreperson managed to get two people to change their votes, but we were still hung. There were still 4 people that voted 'not guilty'.

What now? I asked myself. "I'm ready for a break. Can you see what they are going to do about dinner? Are we going to be stopping for the evening and coming back tomorrow? I am ready to get out of this room."

The Foreperson asked the bailiff about dinner and how late we were supposed to deliberate today, and handed him another note for the judge. She didn't ask it the way I would have. She made it seem like it was no big deal. She obviously didn't have anyone she was in a hurry to get home to, and she didn't need a cigarette.

Did she send another note saying we were hung? Did she ask the judge how we should all vote? Only Gail Whitehead and the Judge could answer that because no one else in the jury room had a clue what was on the notes the two were passing between each other.

The bailiff returned quickly with our answer. "The judge will let you know when you can stop for the night. We can order dinner to be brought in if you like."

"No!" A few shouted.

"You can continue deliberating then."

He shut the door. I don't know about the rest of them, but I got the point. We weren't getting out of there any time soon. *I don't know how long I can hold out. I am trying to stick to my beliefs, but this is getting ridiculous. What do you have to do to get out of this room?* Those thoughts were asked and answered in my head. Reality was setting in. We weren't leaving until we had a unanimous vote. *They aren't going to let us out of here until we find her guilty. That is the only way we can leave this room. Is this how it is supposed to be? Does the system really work like this? Do they keep us hostage until we give them the verdict they want?*

J.L. Hardee

It wasn't long before the dictator laid into the four of us. We were definitely the targets in the room at that point. We were in the minority. It was eight against four. Three of those four were women. I was the only male holding out.

CHAPTER XVIII

I really did not know what to do at that point. *Do they really expect us to compromise our beliefs just to obtain a unanimous verdict?* I kept thinking about what I should do. We weren't instructed on how to handle that type of situation. *Do I ask for clarification from the judge?*

Gail interrupted my thoughts. "We need to discuss this case, and since the four of you don't agree with us, then you need to try to convince us why."

I had enough of this.

"I can tell you why. They have absolutely no physical evidence that ties Kimberly Renee Poole to this murder. There's no murder weapon, no physical evidence, no witnesses that saw her do anything, no witnesses that testified to hearing her conspire with John Boyd Frazier and absolutely no proof that she even told him of their visit. Were there any phone records that showed the two of them talking within the days leading up to this? Were there any phone records showing them talking on the day or night of the murder? NO! There is absolutely no evidence."

"They have her confessing on tape!" Gail stated loudly.

"Ok. Let's discuss her taped confession. To begin with, Kimberly denied any involvement. She denied her involvement for nearly 17 hours straight. The two detectives threatened to take her daughter away from her if she didn't tell them what they wanted to hear. I have been in this room only about 5 hours and I am ready to tell you that I committed the murder if it will let me get out of here. How can we trust anything on that tape with all of the threats and the length of time? They didn't Mirandize her initially and the cops lied to us about why they didn't give her Miranda rights."

"She had an attorney with her." Gail said.

"Ok, let's look at that." I pulled out the transcripts of her confession. It was a very large stack of papers. One can imagine. It was three interviews, one that lasted about 17 hours, and two others that last a long time, too.

I skipped over her first interview. It was the one conducted the night of the murder and it had very little relative information. It was the final two interviews that were material to the matters before us.

"It says that Kimberly arrived at the police station at around 9 p.m. She came with her family attorney. He is not a criminal lawyer by the way." I pointed that out. "Her attorney's name was Victor Lefkowitz. It says that her attorney advised her to cooperate with the police and to answer all of their questions. I have a problem with that to begin with. No attorney in their right mind would tell a client suspected of murder to cooperate with the police and subject them to questions. No criminal attorney would. Not a good one!"

"So what! It's not our fault or the police's fault that she had a bad attorney."

"This girl is no law genius. She didn't know that she had a bad attorney. All she knew is that she was trying to help, and she did what her attorney told her to do."

"He didn't make her confess." Gail stated.

"Well, let's see…."

I scanned through the transcripts. I remembered hearing her attorney asking her questions during the interrogation. It took me a while to find it, but I was able to locate the page.

"Right here, her attorney has said that he is going out of town tomorrow for a trip in Europe. He needs to speed this up. He tells Kimberly that she needs to start telling the police what they want to know. He begins asking her questions in front of the police. Her attorney started acting like a police officer and began interrogating his client in front of two homicide detectives. This isn't right. I can't believe they even allowed this into evidence. Forget that the two cops lied to us. This confession should have never been allowed in this trial. Her attorney was working for the police. He was more worried about his European vacation than protecting his client."

"Did Mr. Lefkowitz ever advise Kimberly to keep her mouth shut? Did he ever tell her that she was free to leave, and she didn't have to speak to the police? Did he ever tell her that she should get a qualified criminal attorney to help her in this matter?"

"NO! This confession should have never been allowed into evidence."

"That's not our place to decide." Gail replied. If the judge allowed it in, we have to consider it as evidence."

"No we don't. The judge told us that, as jurors, we had the right to believe, disbelieve, or dismiss any evidence. I choose to dismiss this evidence. That is my right."

"No it's not." Gail continued.

This became a one-on-one debate; no, a battle between Gail and me.

I took out a piece of blank paper from my notepad. I wrote on it, "We need clarification on the admittance of the confession. Do we have to consider the confession, or can we choose to dismiss it if we believe it was unlawfully obtained or falsely given?"

I passed the piece of paper up to Gail.

J.L. Hardee

"Hand this to the bailiff to give to the judge."

I had folded my note and intended it for the judge to see. It was meant just for the judge. Gail sent a couple of notes to the judge without any of us knowing what was on it. I intended to do the same.

CHAPTER XIX

If anyone guessed that Gail opened my note, they were right. Without hesitation, she opened my note and read it.

"I'm not sending this to the judge. He has been clear on the law."

"Just send it Gail. I want additional clarification for myself."

"No, I'm not sending it."

"You sent a note out to the judge to get clarification on the law as it pertained to circumstantial evidence and conspiracy. You did this without even consulting the rest of us. We didn't even know what you were doing. We all thought we were leaving. What gives you the right?"

"I am the Foreperson!" Gail shouted back.

"So what!"

"I'm not sending it. If I send anything out, it will be a note to tell the judge that you are being unreasonable and refusing to follow the law and his instructions."

Gail Whitehead just threatened me.

"What?" I said.

J.L. Hardee

"You heard me."

"You can't do that."

"If I send a note out, it's going to be to ask that you be removed from this jury and to have one of the alternates seated in your place."

"You can't do that."

"You are refusing to follow the law and the judge's instructions."

"No, I am not! I am following his instructions and just to make sure that I am, I've asked for clarification on his instructions."

I turned my head to the little old lady sitting beside me. I was actually trying hard to hold back tears at this point. I was a grown man, and I was trying not to cry in front of these people. I felt defeated. I was being threatened and I didn't know what to do.

I asked her, "Can she do that? Can she have me removed from the jury?"

She simply replied, "I don't know."

"Will I get in trouble?" I asked softly.

"I don't know."

"What should I do?"

"Just stop talking to her." The little old lady replied.

I was really confused, upset, and I didn't know what to do in this situation. We weren't given instructions on anything regarding who was in charge in the jury room and what our rights as jurors were. We

J.L. Hardee

weren't told that Gail was God, and she was in charge. We weren't told that we had to listen to her. We also weren't told that we weren't. She appeared confident in her knowledge of what to do.

I was getting scared. I felt lost and intimidated. I could definitely see how someone could give a false confession. I was ready to admit that I was the one that shot JFK at this point for sure. If it would get me out of this room, I would say about anything. I hadn't been in this room for 17 hours either. It was working on 6 or 7 at this point. I could only imagine what I'd do after 17 hours of having to listening to Gail Whitehead.

CHAPTER XX

My note never got passed to the judge. I just sat there quietly, feeling defeated. Gail finally decided to let up on me, and she turned her attention to the other three jurors that voted 'not guilty'.

I felt a sense of relief for a moment. I wasn't going to have to argue with her anymore. A million thoughts raced through my head. I thought of my son at home. I wondered what he was doing. I imagined that my wife was cooking dinner, and the two of them were just relaxing at home with no worries in the world. I thought about holding my wife and making love to her.

Then I thought about Gail's threats. *Is she right? Can I really get in trouble?* I didn't know. I was young, dumb, and naïve. I really had no business being on this jury. *Should I ask to be removed? Will I get in trouble if I do? Why is she allowed to pass notes to the Judge and I can't? Does she know him personally?*

J.L. Hardee

A tear dropped from my eye. With it running down my face, I quickly jumped up out of my chair to grab a towel and hoped that no one saw it.

I was a Firefighter. I was an EMT. I had seen some horrific things in my life. I saved people's lives. I had been into raging fires and faced dangers that most people would run from. I had been trapped in a collapsed floor of a mobile home that was burning out of control. I had nearly lost my own life. I survived that. I was a tough guy.

This situation was the toughest that I had ever faced in my life. I was not prepared for this. I had not received any training on this. I knew how to fight a fire. I knew how to give CPR. I knew how to extricate someone from a vehicle.

I just didn't know how to handle this. This situation took my strength from me. This one juror made me feel like a little person that didn't matter. She has made me cry.

This old woman made a young, tough firefighter cry. I remember thinking that to myself. I felt embarrassed and ashamed.

With all these thought running through my head, guess what I wasn't thinking about anymore? Guess what was being ignored.

I wasn't thinking about Kimberly Renee Poole. I wasn't thinking about her rights to a fair trial. I wasn't thinking about my principles. I wasn't thinking about doing what was right. I wasn't thinking about holding the prosecution to their burden of proof. I wasn't thinking about this case at all.

All I wanted to do was get out of that room. I began gnawing on my fingers. They were almost to the cuticles. They were looking like nubs. If only I had a cigarette to help relax me.

A valium would have been even better. I was really stressing. I can't imagine what the other 3 jurors were thinking. They saw me get beat down to nothing. Then, they were the targets of Gail. How were they going to hold up? What were they going to say to her?

I can honestly say that I wasn't paying Gail or any of the other jurors any attention at this point. Gail was talking to two of the ladies that voted 'not guilty', but I couldn't even hear them. I had tuned them out. My mind was racing, and my thoughts were anywhere, but this room. I have no idea what Gail said to them or if she threatened them too. I could only imagine.

CHAPTER XXI

It has been nearly 12 years since that trial and that day, and the thought of what happened in that room still brings me to tears.

I don't know if my conclusions were right. I don't know if my stance was right. I don't know if my principles were right. At the time, I thought I was doing what was right. I was following the law, as I saw it. I was holding the prosecution to their burden of proof.

A woman's life was on the line. We owed her that much. What if it was one of your loved ones on trial? What if it was you on trial? What if you were innocent? Don't you want the jury to follow their hearts and their principles? Wouldn't you want the jury to hold the prosecution to their burden of proof? Wouldn't you want them to be sure of guilt before they sent you away for the rest of your life?

Do you want the jury speculating on your guilt? Do you want the jury to just believe the cops because the prosecution says you should? Do you want the jury to believe the police after they had lied under oath in a court of law? Do you want them to throw out those little lies and over look them and just accept everything else they said? Police officers are human too. Are we to just trust everything they say just because they wear a badge?

I wore a badge, too. I also took an oath to protect the public. That doesn't mean I'm God, and that doesn't mean that these guys were either.

I had to do what was right. I had to follow my conscious.

Didn't I?

Shouldn't I?

Over the next hour, I just sat there with all of these thoughts turning through my head. I didn't have the answers. I wanted to seek guidance from someone in authority. I asked to get clarification from the judge. That was denied to me. There was one person that could give me the guidance I needed, and I wasn't allowed to speak to him.

The other 'guilty' voters were just sitting at the table listening to Gail speak with two of the jurors. They didn't even express their opinions or try to sway the others' votes. They left that all up to Gail. Why shouldn't they? She put me down in no time. She made me cry. They didn't need to do anything but sit back and let Gail dictate her way.

J.L. Hardee

Aren't jurors entitled to their own opinions? Do we all have to think the same? Should we all vote the way Gail Whitehead does just because she says so?

Aren't you glad you weren't the defendant in this case? It wasn't looking good for her at this point, and it had nothing to do with her innocence or guilt.

As my thoughts continued, they were suddenly interrupted.

I overheard Gail say to one the jurors again, "This girl is a stripper and a lying cheat. She is a nasty slut. She doesn't deserve freedom. She deserves to rot in jail the rest of her life."

Wow!

That really got my attention. It turned personal. *Gail doesn't care if this girl is actually guilty of the crime she has been charged with. She hates this girl because of her lifestyle. Gail must have been scorned at one point in her life. She is really taking this personally. She wants this girl to spend the rest of her days in a 6'x 9' cell just because she worked as a stripper and she cheated on her husband.*

I wander what Gail wants for me. I cheated on my wife before. My wife had cheated on me. Should we both be in prison for that? I have never been a stripper, but I had my bachelor party at a strip club. Should I be sent to prison, because I have watched a stripper before?

I wanted to interrupt Gail and say something about her comments. I wanted to tell the other jurors to stop listening to that nonsense. I was a coward though. Gail turned a once brave firefighter into a coward. I was scared to speak up. I didn't want her lashing back out at me. I had managed to sit here in a little bit of peace for the last few moments. Was I ready to be back in the hot seat? Was I ready to see what Gail would do to me next?

I decided not. I never spoke up. I allowed the nonsense to continue. I tuned them out again. I knew that these two jurors didn't stand a chance against Gail. They were too reserved. They were too polite. I wasn't brave enough to come to their defense, and I was thankful Gail's misguided thoughts weren't being directed at me anymore.

I don't care what happens. I'm still not changing my vote. Let Gail do whatever she wants with these other two jurors. There are still two of us voting 'not guilty'. The little old lady sitting next to me was on my side. She wouldn't give in to Gail. She is older than Gail and she won't put up with any of the nonsense that I had to.

It wasn't long before the other young male juror spoke up. "Let's take another vote and see where we are at now."

CHAPTER XXII

Gail stopped her conversation with the two jurors. She turned to face forward and said, "Let's vote."

She looked to her right and the jury began announcing their votes out loud.

"Guilty!"

"Guilty!"

"Guilty!"

"Guilty!"

"Guilty!"

"Not Guilty!"

"Not Guilty!"

"Guilty!"

"Guilty!"

"Guilty!"

"Guilty!"

"Guilty!"

J.L. Hardee

The look of disappointment had to be visible on my face. Gail managed to convince the other two jurors to change their votes. It wasn't because the girl was guilty, but because she was a stripper and a slut in their eyes.

The vote was 10-2.

Gail skipped right over me and turned her attention to the nice, little, old lady.

"What about you?"

"I'm not changing my vote." She said.

"We're all ready to get out of here and go home." Gail explained.

"Well, you better tell the judge that we're hung then and ask if we can be done or if we can retire for the evening and just continue tomorrow."

"I am not asking if we can go back to the motel for another night just to continue this tomorrow. There are only two of you that are keeping us here. I don't want to have to be here another day just because the two of you won't do what's right."

"Then tell the Judge we are hung." I added.

"No, I'm not." Gail laid back into her. She was showing some true skills as a dictator. She really should have been a drill sergeant.

The woman quietly said, "You better just send a note to the judge telling him we're hung and that we aren't going to be changing our minds."

Gail looked like she was going to give in. She wrote something down on a piece of paper. She handed the paper to the bailiff.

Again, I have no idea what the paper said. I don't know if Gail told the judge we were hung or if she just told him that we wanted to continue until we dropped. There's no telling what the note said. I didn't trust Gail, and with her obvious bias, I wouldn't put it past her to do anything. Did she tell the Judge we were hung?

The bailiff returned pretty quickly. "You can just continue deliberating. The judge will let you know when you can stop."

What? What does that mean? What did Gail say to them? Shouldn't we get to know what she said? Shouldn't we get a say? What do they want us to do?

There were so many emotions running through me. I was tired now. I was actually physically and mentally exhausted. It was nearly 8 p.m. We had been up since 6 a.m. and we had been in that jury room for nearly 9 hours without a break.

"We are all ready to go home and the two of you are keeping us from leaving!" Gail shouted at our direction.

"Fine!" The quiet, polite, little old lady spoke up. "I will change my vote if that makes you happy and it gets us out of here. I'm tired and I don't care anymore."

Oh my God! This has nothing to do with innocence or guilt anymore. We haven't discussed the case in awhile. This is all about getting out of here now. It's obvious that the judge will not let us leave until we make a unanimous decision and there is no chance of getting Gail to change her mind.

The little old lady gave up. She left me sitting all alone. It's was 11 against 1. Little ole me is sitting all by myself in this room, and all eyes were on me.

I stood and walked to the window. I opened the window and took a well-needed breath of fresh air. I just sat there staring out into the darkness. Everything was so eerily quiet. My back was turned to the jury, but I knew they were all looking at me.

What do I do? I don't believe the State proved their case. I don't believe we should convict someone on lies. I don't believe there was enough evidence to make a decision. I am supposed to vote 'not guilty' under those circumstances. Aren't I? Aren't I supposed to stand up for my beliefs?

All of these questions were stirring through me. Another tear poured from my eyes. I didn't even care anymore if anyone saw me crying. I

J.L. Hardee

wiped my face as my nose began to run. I was really upset and beating myself up. I was questioning myself. I didn't know what to do.

One of the female jurors stood and came over to me. If it had been Gail, I would have been charged with murder, because I would have tossed her out of that two-story window.

The juror put her hand on my back. She kind of turned me towards her. It was the female juror that had been one of the earlier split votes.

She tried to comfort me. She said, "It is ok. Just take a few minutes to yourself. It's okay if you cry. This girl is guilty, and you shouldn't be upset," she said. "We are all tired and ready to go home. The rest of the jurors think she's guilty. If you aren't sure what to do then just follow our lead."

I started shaking my head in disbelief. I thought she was going to tell me that it was ok for me to stand by my beliefs; that I didn't have to give in. She never said that. She was just using a different tactic on me than Gail. She was trying to be sneaky by acting like she cared how I felt.

I sucked up the water running from my eyes and nose and turned around to face the jurors.

"I don't believe this girl did this. I don't believe the two detectives that lied to us. I am not going to change my mind. I am not going to change my vote."

J.L. Hardee

"I am going to see if the judge will have him removed from the jury." Gail stated out loud.

"No, don't do that, you may get us all in trouble." One man stated.

"Why don't we just tell the judge that we are hopelessly deadlocked? We can let another jury decide this case at a later date."

"We've tried that." Gail explained. "We got nowhere trying that. The judge and the State don't want to go to the expense of having to try this case again just because you won't listen to reasoning. You're failing to use your common sense." Gail said. "No one would confess to something they didn't do."

"Yes they would!" I shouted. "I would tell you about anything to get out of this room, and I haven't been interrogated by two seasoned homicide detectives."

"Great then!"

"Vote guilty and we can all leave right now!"

"Fine, you win!"

That's all I said. We didn't take another vote. We didn't do a round table to confirm the vote. Gail wrote out another note and passed it to the bailiff. She began filling out the Charge sheets. None of us knew what she wrote on that note either.

She didn't even confirm with me that I was willing to vote 'guilty'.

It was about 8:45 p.m. We had been in that room since noon. I really didn't care anymore. I just felt defeated. The truth didn't matter to me anymore. The burden of proof didn't matter. Right and wrong didn't matter. Justice didn't matter. All that matter was that I got out of this room and away from Gail Whitehead.

It seemed like it took forever for the bailiff to return.

J.L. Hardee

CHAPTER XXIII

When the bailiff returned to the room, everyone was standing. I was still by the window. I was trying to wipe the tears away before I had to step back out into that courtroom.

"Have you completed the papers as the judge instructed," the bailiff asked. "Is your verdict unanimous?"

"Yes." Gail replied.

I wanted so badly to speak up right then and yell, "NO". I was too afraid. I didn't know what would happen to me if I did, and all I really wanted was to get out of there. I could care less what happened to Kimberly Renee Poole at that point.

The female juror that had tried to comfort me leaned in and whispered in my ear. "She won't get that much time since she wasn't the one that pulled the trigger."

That eased my mind just a bit. I was the last one out of that room that night, even though I was the first one that wanted to be out of that room.

J.L. Hardee

As we walked across the room to the jury box and passed by the defendant, I couldn't even look at her. I held my head down, as I walked slowly and deliberately to my seat. We were all seated. I didn't even dare look around the room. I just stared at the floor in front of me.

"Has the jury reached a unanimous verdict?"

"Yes, your Honor." Gail replied, as she stood.

"Please pass your verdict slip to the bailiff."

The bailiff handed the verdict slip to the judge. He quickly glance at it and passed it back.

"Will the defendant please rise?"

"Madam Clerk, will you announce the verdict, please?"

"The State of South Carolina vs. Kimberly Renee Poole as to count one on the indictment, murder, the verdict is 'GUILTY'."

I looked up at the clerk with tears in my eyes. I just couldn't control it. I wasn't strong enough to hold them back. She just continued without a break in between.

"As to count two of the indictment, conspiracy, the verdict is 'GUILTY'."

I never looked at Kimberly Renee Poole. I was too ashamed. I have no idea what her response was. I kept my head held down. I was hoping the reporters weren't taking my picture with me crying.

J.L. Hardee

Defense Attorney, William Isaac Diggs, broke the silence in the room. "I want the jury polled, Your Honor."

The judge faced the jury, and I looked up with fear in my eyes as to what was going to happen next.

"Each of you, please stand and tell us if this is your verdict."

Gail was the first to rise.

"Yes, your Honor!" she shouted.

One by one each juror stood and said, "Yes."

When they got to me, my knees were trembling. I was scared to death. *What do I do? What happens if I say no? Will I get in trouble? Will I be going to jail? Will I be taken away from my family?*

The cowardice in me came out again, as I rose up from my seat. I didn't even look up. I surely wasn't going to look toward the defendant. I quietly said," yes." I can't even believe they heard me because I spoke so softly trying to force that word out of me.

That was it. That was your Justice.

CHAPTER XXIV

The judge turned to the jury and spoke to us. I can't even remember exactly what he said. I wasn't really paying attention. I know he thanked us for our service. He told us we could leave or we could stay to hear the sentencing.

I wanted to leave for 9 hours or more. I wasn't even thinking about a cigarette anymore. I was ashamed and I felt really torn up inside. I had to stay to listen to the fate of the defendant. All of the jurors got up to leave. The only ones that stayed were Gail and me. Of course, Gail was going to stay; she had just railroaded this girl into prison single handedly.

The judge gave Brent Poole's family a chance to speak before sentencing. I watched them, as they stepped forward, but I never heard what they said. My mind was on my own faults at that point. After the victim's family spoke, the judge continued.

"Kimberly Renee Poole, please rise."

J.L. Hardee

The judge gave a little speech to Kimberly Renee Poole, saying something about how disgusted he was with her. I don't even remember his exact words. What I do remember is...."You will be confined to the State Department of Corrections for the rest of your natural life."

What? I thought. *For the rest of her life?* I didn't even hear the judge when he added an additional 5 years concurrent for the conspiracy charge.

Life? Her entire life?

That juror told me that she wouldn't get much time since she wasn't the one that pulled the trigger. Boy was she wrong.

I finally looked up at Kimberly Renee Poole. She appeared devastated. *This was my fault. I was a coward. I failed my duties.*

As the judge dismissed the court, I stood up and walked toward the defense table. *I am going to go tell this lawyer what happened. I have to tell him what happened in that jury room.* I was determined. I was going to fix this. I was going to make this right. I was going to let them know how we were bullied into changing our verdicts. I was going to let them know that the jury was hung, and we were forced to change our verdicts just so we could get a break from that room.

As I approached the defense table, Judge Edward Cottingham called out my name in open court. "Sir, I would like to see you in my chambers."

J.L. Hardee

The judge brought in the attorney's from both sides. I was scared to death. He asked me if I had some issues.

I immediately, without hesitation said "Yes, Your Honor."

I told him that we were hung and that I didn't want to change my vote. "I voted not guilty," I remember saying.

"It's too late now." He said.

He brought up the fact that I had a misdemeanor conviction and asked me if I faced more than 30 days in jail for that and I said no. I was getting really scared at that point. The judge asked the attorney's to step out so he could speak to me alone.

My knees really began to shake. Tears poured from my eyes. There was no hiding them. I had no idea what he was going to do to me.

After the attorneys left the room, the judge came closer to me. He put his hand on my shoulder.

"Son, I can see you are beating yourself up with what happened. Don't. You don't need to. You made the right decision."

That was it. He opened the door and stepped to the side and directed me out.

"There are a lot of reporters outside and that Court TV, and they want to interview the jurors."

"I don't want to speak to them, Your Honor."

"You don't have to. I'll have the bailiff walk you to your car."

J.L. Hardee

CHAPTER XXV

As I drove home that night, it was all I could do to calm myself. I smoked two cigarettes back to back. I was driving through downtown Conway heading back towards Loris when I heard a siren behind me. I looked up and saw a Police car on my tail.

What now? What did I do? Are they going to send me to jail for trying to stand up for my beliefs in that jury room? Are they going to try to stop me from telling the truth about what happened in there?

The thoughts were scaring me, as I pulled over. I hadn't made it more than a mile from the courthouse.

As the officer approached, I could see that it was a City of Conway Police Officer.

He said, "Sir, where are you coming from tonight?"

"I just left the courthouse. I was one of the jurors on the murder trial." I explained.

"Ok, I'm sorry to have bothered you. I am sure you are ready to get home. I pulled you over because one of your head lights is out. You can go now. Please take care of that head light."

He never even asked to see my drivers' license. He obviously knew about the case and knew that the jury had just been released. Who would lie about being on a jury for a capital murder case?

I didn't even call my wife to let her know I was on my way home. It was about 10 p.m. or so, and I didn't even want to speak to her. Besides, she was probably in bed by then. I knew my son would be.

The town was quiet. The streets were void of any people. As I turned on my street, I was just hoping that I would be able to go to sleep that night.

The judge put my mind at ease just a bit. He told me that I made the right decision. Maybe he knew something that I didn't. Maybe there was a piece of evidence that he was aware of that hadn't been presented at trial. From his comments to the defendant when he was sentencing her and his comments to me after the trial, it was obvious that his mind was made up a long time ago.

Judge Cottingham was a smart man with a lot of years of experience doing this. Maybe I should just trust his words and not worry about this anymore.

The lights appeared to be off at my house.

J.L. Hardee

My wife must be asleep. I am going to have to sneak in without trying to wake anyone.

As I walked through the carport, the garage light turned on. She was standing there with the door open.

"I saw you pull in. I just put Justin to bed. How did it go?"

"Don't ask." I said.

The tears were gone. They were all dried up, and I was relaxed finally. I was home. I just shook my head when my wife asked how it went.

"Your mom called. She was just checking in to see if you had made it back and what had happened."

I sat down on the couch and she asked me if I wanted a cup of coffee or Mt. Dew. I agreed to the coffee. I lit up a cigarette. We were both smokers, and while we didn't smoke in the same room with our son, we smoked in the house. It was really nice to sit and enjoy a cigarette on my own couch.

"Here's your coffee. You should call your mom."

"Ok. Can you bring me the phone?"

I really didn't feel like talking to my mom. I was ashamed of what just happened, and I really didn't want to tell anyone about it. I surely wasn't ready to talk about it. I dreaded that phone call. I knew she was going to ask.

J.L. Hardee

It was the first thing out of her mouth after hello. She skipped the 'how are you doing'. She went right for the juice.

"Well, what was the verdict?"

"Guilty! Guilty on both counts!"

"Oh, so she did do it?"

My mom wasn't going to let it just go with that. I knew she was going to pry for details.

"I don't know if she did it or not."

"What?"

"And you voted 'guilty?'"

"Yes, I voted guilty."

"Why would you vote guilty if you don't know if she did it or not?"

"I don't know mom. I just don't know."

"That's not good enough son. You need to tell me what happened."

She wasn't going to quit. My mom was an avid reader, and a crime enthusiast. She read all the true crime novels and mystery books as soon as they were published.

I took a sip of my coffee and prepared myself for a very long conversation. Then I realized... this is a long distance call. "Mom, can you call me right back? It's going to take me a while to explain this to you."

Page133

She didn't even give me time to go the bathroom. She called right back.

I had no choice but to explain my actions. I told her everything that happened that day in the jury room and with the judge after the proceedings.

After listening intently to everything I said, my mom stated her peace.

"That's not right. You should've held your ground. They couldn't have done anything to you for not being willing to change your vote. What the judge said to you after the trial was wrong too. He was obviously biased and shouldn't have been on the case. Do you know that the head juror sent the notes out telling him you were hung?"

"Well, I saw her hand a note to the bailiff a few different times. I don't know what was on them, but when he returned he told us to continue to deliberate."

"So, the judge obviously forced you to make a decision. That is why he denied your breaks. He knew if you were all stuck in that room long enough and he didn't let you out that you'd be forced to compromise. He did that on purpose. Does the defense attorney know?"

"I tried to tell him after the trial, and that's when the judge called me into his chambers." I explained.

"You have to do something."

J.L. Hardee

"You need to call the defense attorney first thing tomorrow, and you need to tell him what happened. Don't forget to tell him about the threats from the other juror about having you removed and stuff. Don't forget to tell him that you asked for clarification on the law, and she refused to send it to the judge."

"Ok! I will call him tomorrow, and I'll tell him."

"Alright! Try to get some sleep. It sounds like you are exhausted."

"I am."

"Ok. Goodnight!"

We hung up the phone. I didn't even realize it, but my wife had been sitting there listening to our entire conversation, which lasted over an hour.

"Your mom is right. You need to do something about this. You can't get in any trouble for telling the truth."

My wife and I went to bed. I didn't even feel like making love anymore. We just snuggled together and I fell asleep pretty quickly.

CHAPTER XXVI

I woke up to the sunlight the following morning. I had the day off, so I hadn't set my alarm. Surprisingly, I slept like a baby all night. I must've really been spent. I normally don't sleep well when I'm stressed or have something on my mind.

I took a shower and enjoyed a cup of coffee and a cigarette sitting in my chair. I temporarily forgot about the drama from the day before. My wife was right behind me though. As soon as she walked in the living room, she asked me if I was going to call that lawyer this morning.

"It's 7 a.m. Lawyers probably work banker hours. Their office probably won't open until 9 a.m."

"Why don't you just look them up and try? If they don't answer you can leave a message for him."

I called William Diggs shortly after 7 a.m. the following morning after the trial. A woman's voice answered the phone. I was actually very surprised that someone answered that early.

"Can I speak to Mr. Diggs please?"

J.L. Hardee

"May I ask who is calling?"

As soon as I told her my name, she said, "Hang on. He is right here. He will want to speak with you."

"This is Bill Diggs." He said.

"I just wanted to let you know that we were a hung jury and I tried to hold out. I asked for notes to be sent out to the judge."

He immediately asked if I could come in to his office. He didn't want to discuss this by phone. I asked him when.

"Now," He said. "If not, I can come out to you."

I agreed to come into his office later that morning. He was all the way down in Myrtle Beach. It was going to be a 40 minute drive for me. They didn't have all of the new highways with quick access to the beach yet. I was going to have to drive right back through Conway and pass near that courthouse to go see him. I wasn't really looking forward to it.

I gathered up my notes that I took during the trial. We were allowed to keep them. It was a long drive to the beach thinking about the events of the previous day.

I thought my visit with Mr. Diggs would just be an informal conversation in his office.

I was wrong. When I arrived, Mr. Diggs had his conference room set up with a recorder. He directed me to a sit and asked if I needed some coffee or anything. I agreed to a cup of coffee and sat down nervously.

J.L. Hardee

Three people from that office sat across the table from me. I think one was Mr. Diggs' son and the other was a legal secretary. Mr. Diggs and his secretary both had note pads in hand.

"Sir, do you mind if we record this conversation?"

I had nothing to hide, and although I was ashamed of my actions in that jury room, I intended to stand up and face this problem head-on. I was going to be a man about it and just tell the truth. I didn't know if I'd face any trouble or not, and by this point I didn't care anymore.

I agreed to allow them to record my visit.

I handed him my note pad.

"What is this?"

"It's my notes that I took during the trial. I even jotted down some things in the jury room about the foreperson. I think you will find my notes interesting."

I explained to Mr. Diggs my position; that I had voted 'not guilty'. I told him the reasons why I had chose that vote. I informed him that I thought the two detectives lied. I asked for my notes back, and I read the questions and the detective's answers to him. "I thought these were lies," I explained.

He agreed and told me that was why he asked them those questions. He said the recorded statements should have never been allowed into court.

I continued and gave him a full account of what happened in that jury room. When I was done speaking, he asked me a few questions for clarification, and we were done. My statement with him took about 2-3 hours.

I asked him if I could step out and smoke.

"Sure." He said. "I won't be like the judge and deny you a break."

Mr. Diggs stepped outside with me that day.

He then informed me that there were things about the case that the jury never got to hear. He said that his investigator uncovered evidence of a 3rd parties' guilt, but the judge refused to allow the testimony in because it would paint a bad light on the Myrtle Beach Police Department.

He told me of an email that John Boyd Frasier had sent to a friend a few days prior to the event. In this email, John told his friend that Renee had refused to speak to him and refused to let him know where Brent was so that he could beat his ass.

"What? You mean there was evidence that Renee didn't conspire with him, that he may have done this on his own?"

"Yes!"

"What's even worse than that is that the police had this evidence. They knew about it before trial and we were not allowed to present it.

J.L. Hardee

This was a high profile case and the Myrtle Beach Police were not going to admit to any mistakes with Court TV around."

"That sucks! Well, what now?"

"I will try to appeal." He said.

"Ok!" I left it at that. I assumed that he'd be able to get this reversed immediately. I left there feeling pretty good.

The Horry County courtroom, where the trial of Kimberly Renee Poole was held. This main courtroom, in the old courthouse is now used for traffic court.

Jury Room used in Kimberly Renee Poole murder trial. This small room is now used as an employee break room.

Brent and Kimberly Renee Poole on their wedding day in 1995.

Kimberly Renee Poole with daughter, Katie, when she was 2 years old, June 1998. Photo taken in Myrtle Beach, during family's vacation, just prior to the murder of Brent Poole.

Kimberly Renee Poole with daughter, Katie, now 16. Brent Poole's parents kept Katie from seeing her mother for 14 years. This photo was taken at Leath Correctional Institute when they were reunited. Katie now lives with Renee's parents and is able to visit and communicate with her mother regularly.

J.L. Hardee

Kimberly Renee Poole and daughter, Katie on their first Christmas together after being separated for 14 years.)

Photos provided by Marie Summey, mother of Kimberly Renee Poole.

AFTERTHOUGHT

It was 1999 when Kimberly Renee Poole was convicted of the murder of Brent Poole. Her initial appeal was heard by Judge Cottingham in the days following her trial. He immediately denied her appeal, and it appeared, without any thought or review of the evidence presented to him.

After the trial, the defense discovered that Jury Foreperson Gail Whitehead went to church with the chief prosecutor, Solicitor J. Gregory Hembree. Neither Hembree nor Whitehead revealed this before the trial. We were specifically asked, under oath, by the Judge if we knew any of the parties related to the case. We were asked if we knew the DA's or defense team. I wasn't present during her questioning, but she obviously lied about that. Whitehead and Hembree later admitted knowing each other from church, but denied having a personal relationship or friendship with each other. Defense Attorney Diggs filed an appeal

J.L. Hardee

based on this information for Juror misconduct and Prosecutorial misconduct. That appeal was denied.

No charges have ever been filed against Jury Foreperson Gail Whitehead, Detective John King, or Detective Terry Altman for perjury in relation to this case.

All of Kimberly Renee Poole's subsequent appeals were also denied. Her last appeal to the Supreme Court was denied, because her attorney, William Isaac Diggs, failed to file the motion in a timely manner. The matter was dismissed and wasn't even heard by the Supreme Court. After this mistake, Poole fired her defense team, and has been seeking new counsel.

Kimberly Renee Poole is currently imprisoned at Leath Correctional Institute in Greenwood, SC. Barring a miracle from God; she will spend the rest of her life there.

With the way politics and corruption are in our government, I don't ever foresee Kimberly Renee Poole receiving a fair and impartial jury or the light of day again.

It has been 12 years since her conviction, and I've tried to forget about the mistakes that I made in that jury room. I can't forget it though. That one day is a day that will haunt me for the rest of my life.

I hope you never have to sit on a jury and more than that, I hope you don't ever have your fate in the hands on 12 jurors.

J.L. Hardee

I've made many mistakes in my life. Some of those mistakes have cost me dearly. In recent years, I've changed my life, and I'm trying my best to make up for mistakes I made. I can only hope that this story will bring to light the injustice that took place in that Jury Room. I can only hope that this never happens to someone again. I can only hope that judges will stop forcing jurors to make a decision. If the jury is hung, leave it that way. Don't force them to give up their beliefs just to close a case.

Finally, I hope that this story finds itself in the hands of an accomplished attorney, judge, or politician that cares more about doing what's right than what is popular. If this was your loved one, wouldn't you want them to have had a fair jury? Would you want them to rot in jail and be forgotten? What if she didn't do it?

The jury in this case was split 6-6 for hours. Kimberly Renee Poole wasn't found guilty, because the jury thought she committed this crime. She was found guilty because she was a stripper, she cheated on her husband and we were ready to go home. She was found guilty because I wasn't mature enough, educated enough, or strong enough to stand up for my beliefs.

Kimberly Renee Poole should have had a hung jury that day. She sits in a jail cell the rest of her life and leaves behind a daughter that is now 16 years old.

J.L. Hardee

Please visit my profiles below for updates and new releases. My next book, 'My Sweet Revenge', is planned for release in early 2013.

https://www.smashwords.com/profile/view/hardeejl

https://www.facebook.com/J.L.HARDEE.AUTHOR

J.L. Hardee